TOWERING TALES & A RIPPING YARN

Yorkshire football's grassroots legends

By Steven Penny

ISBN: 9798787897586

Cover pictures:
Front, main image: Action from England's most scenic football ground –
Richmond Town's Earls Orchard.
Others – from left – Michael Palin's Barnestoneworth United shirt, Joe Harvey
(Edlington and Newcastle United), Frank Worthington (Littletown and England),
Denis Law (Littletown and Scotland), Dominic Calvert-Lewin (Handsworth and
England), Paul Heaton (Sculcoates Amateurs and Beautiful South) and Keith
Hackett (Penistone and Euro Championships).

Back, main image: Game over. Littletown volunteer Colin Bould returns the
club's ball-gathering equipment at the end of the match.
Others – from Left - Alan Warboys (Goldthorpe and Bristol Rovers), Geoff
Horsfield (Athersley Rec and Birmingham City), George Robledo (Brampton
Ellis School and World Cup finals), Arthur Wharton (Yorkshire Main and world's
first black professional footballer), Mark Jones (Wombwell and Busby Babe) and
Gordon Banks (Rawmarsh Welfare and England World Cup winner).

steve@stevepennymedia.co.uk

A Penny For Your Sports Production

CONTENTS

X marks the spot: A common sight at grounds across the country during the 2020/21 season.

INTRODUCTION

2020 was a year unlike any other. The coronavirus pandemic wrecked lives and businesses on a global scale.

Unsurprisingly, football was affected, with the 2019/20 season curtailed and the 2020/21 instalment stuttering to a halt barely weeks after it had begun.

While the 'elite' clubs managed to play on, it was in front of empty stadiums and with regular postponements due to positive Covid-19 tests.

It meant I was left at a loose end for many match days and it gave me time to re-release my 2003 book, Soap Stars and Burst Bubbles – A season of Yorkshire football.

It came after I had managed to get round a few clubs between Covid closures and posted features on the Tyke Travels Facebook page. The interest generated brought renewed interest in my 'groundhopping' days.

I had initially planned to revisit those clubs to publish an updated volume but the declaration of most of their leagues null and void blew that one out of the water. Alternative plans to focus on how clubs were coping after shutdown were also ended when the second lockdown arrived.

Instead I decided to produce a completely new book, again based on Yorkshire clubs. It saw me travel to clubs below the normal level at which I watch my football. That gave me chance to tell their tales – and what stories they were. Despite often playing at a level of football barely discernible with a telescope from the rarefied atmosphere of the Premier League, there slowly emerged the fact that many of these clubs had being a stepping stone to greatness for a variety of players.

Denis Law, Frank Worthington, Gordon Banks, Dean Windass and Dominic Calvert-Lewin all shone on the playing fields of Yorkshire, while managers Bill Shankly, Herbert Chapman and Joe Harvey learned their trade in the Broad Acres.

However, those featured are not all the 'normal' legends – these are also the unsung heroes and those whose contribution to the game has perhaps been overlooked.

Enjoy your trip around some of Yorkshire's lesser-known clubs and the part they have played in this beautiful game of ours.

Steven Penny,

South Elmsall, summer 2021

1. SHIELDS ARE UP

Friday, August 7, 2020
Hough Lane, Wombwell
Wombwell Main 2 Dodworth MW 3
It's OK to Talk Shield

A first chance to witness some on-field action in the 2020/21 season and I managed to find a 'competitive' fixture. With clubs slowly coming out of their coronavirus-induced hibernation, August 1 had seen a return to the pitch in 'friendly' action for many teams, thanks to a relaxation of Government rules on spectators at football matches.

However, that only applied to the seventh level of non-League football and below and, within days, had been amended to an even lower level. Thankfully, at clubs below the Northern Counties East League, most grounds are not enclosed so matches were allowed and I managed to grab a slice of the action for the first It's OK to Talk Shield encounter between Wombwell Main and Dodworth Miners Welfare at Hough Lane.

The match was in aid of Barnsley Samaritans and Project14DV and attracted a decent-sized 'gathering of interested passers-by' – supporters are not allowed, of course – numbering around 100. Cameras were banned, although the official club photographer was allowed to take a few, which he made available for a reasonable price to anyone wishing to get a memento of the clash.

Although Wombwell Main have a long history, dating back to at least the turn of the 20th Century, their ground is basic, consisting of a pitch surround, two smart dug-outs and advertising hoardings on a neighbour's fence. They first entered the FA Cup in 1906, playing 10 ties, despite never having played above Sheffield & Hallamshire County Senior League level. They have four league titles to their name since 1998, as well as three league cups, but throughout the last century played second fiddle to neighbours Wombwell Town. That club had played in the Yorkshire League in various guises but folded in 2000, reforming 18 years later and now playing at the town's Recreation Ground.

Main share their facilities with the cricket club across the playing field and the clubhouse was heaving with all outside space taken. A steady stream of beer from there to the pitch was supplemented with trays of fish and chips from the neighbouring chippy as families enjoyed the chance to picnic on the glorious summer's evening. The entrance to the club's changing rooms contains a plaque, commemorating Wombwell-born Busby Babe Mark Jones. He was killed in 1958 at the age of 24 in the Munich Air Disaster and is fondly remembered in the town. He was a regular at training sessions at the "Hough Lane Stadium" before the big-time beckoned and as a youngster had played for Darfield Foulstone School and Don & Dearne Schoolboys, eventually making it to Barnsley Boys, where he was spotted by a Manchester United scout.

At Old Trafford, the "seam of Yorkshire granite", stood between marauding centre forwards and the United goal, helping the Red Devils to the league title in 1956 and 1957. He missed the 1957 FA Cup final defeat to Aston Villa due to an eye injury. According The Busby Babe blog, Jones was the archetypal pivot "broad of beam, crushing in the tackle and majestic in the air".

However, he was as gentle a footballer as you could find, rarely spotted off the field without his trademark pipe and always keen to talk about his beloved budgerigars. On the pitch he was in a regular battle for a starting berth with Jackie Blanchflower but there was no malice between the pair, indeed Blanchflower was best man at Jones' 1954 wedding to June Conry in Staincross.

Jones was working as a bricklayer when he moved across the Pennines, after impressing as captain of England Schoolboys. He made his first-team debut for United at the age of 17 in a home victory over Sheffield Wednesday but had to wait four years to become a regular after appearing about 120 times for the reserves, going on to make 121 first-team appearances, scoring just one goal – the winner against Birmingham City at Old Trafford in the last home game before Christmas 1955 He was called up for England and was tipped to succeed Billy Wright at the heart of defence but never gained a full cap.

Jones had played in a 3-3 European Cup draw against Red Star

Belgrade in Yugoslavia in February 1958. The aeroplane taking the team back to Manchester stopped at Munich for refuelling but tragedy struck when it tried to take off in slushy conditions. At the third attempt, it crashed through a fence, went across a road and into a house. Twenty-three people perished, including Barnsley-born Tommy Taylor and other United players Geoff Bent, Roger Byrne, Eddie Colman, Duncan Edwards (who died in hospital 15 days later), David Pegg and Billy Whelan. Other casualties were the club's chief coach Bert Whalley, secretary Walter Crickmer, trainers Bert Whalley and Tom Curry and former England and Manchester City goalkeeper Frank Swift, who was a journalist for the News of the World. Seven more journalists lost their lives with other passengers critically injured, including manager Matt Busby. Of the 44 people on board, only 21 survived.

Jones was buried in Wombwell, leaving his wife, who was pregnant with his daughter – Lynne, born four months later – and two-year-old son Gary.

Back at Wombwell and two pitch side benches, commemorating former supporters, are immaculately presented with fresh flowers in vases. Despite the basic facilities at the ground, fans do have an elevated view of proceedings, from grass banking behind the dug-outs. The pitch itself is on a plateau, with the goal line at shoulder height as you walk behind the net. Behind the far goal is open countryside, while the nearside touchline consists of a grass path, separated from the pitch by a barrier, with the advertising hoardings behind.

Today's combatants are both in the Premier Division of the Sheffield & Hallamshire County Senior League but it was the visitors who looked the classier outfit, despite the home ranks boasting prolific non-League scorer Danny Frost. The red-and-black striped visitors took the lead after nine minutes when their left winger stormed down the touchline and pulled the ball back but no one was able to convert. However, the ball was not cleared and man of the match Liam Owen found space to tuck the ball inside the post. The goalkeeper's admission of guilt turned into a blame game all in one sentence" "I know I dropped a b@!!@ck but that 'C' shouldn't have been able to shoot from there," he berated his defenders

A mid-half drinks break provided the refreshment needed for Dodworth to double their advantage. With 25 minutes gone, a home defender pushed Dodworth's No.11 right in front of the linesman, who flagged for a penalty, with the referee unsighted. Owen stepped up to send the goalkeeper the wrong way for his second goal. Wombwell thought they had grabbed a lifeline six minutes later when a shot was well saved but the loose ball fell for the Greens centre forward to tap home. Unfortunately for him, the flag was already up for offside. It all looked to be over seven minutes before the interval when the hosts failed to make inroads after a prolonged attack and a quick break caught them out with a driven ball into the area, seeing Jack Owen join his brother on the scoresheet to make it 3-0.

The second half was much of the same with the visitors dominating possession but unable to add to their tally and it almost proved costly. Liam Owen should have completed his hat-trick on the hour-mark when he was gifted the ball on the edge of the penalty area but he tucked his shot wide of the goal with the goalkeeper beaten. Jack Owen was then denied by an acrobatic clearance off the line before a substitute was ordered to "Hit it! Hit it" from fully 35 yards out. He did as demanded and only a finger-tip save from the fast back-pedalling home goalkeeper kept out his effort. Another drinks break proved invigorating for the hosts who suddenly found their way to goal. Frost pulled one back after 75 minutes and, with two minutes remaining, got on the end of a free-kick to make it 3-2.

Frost once scored 14 goals in a 28-0 win for Wombwell in a Barnsley Sunday Cup match but the former Ossett Town, Shaw Lane and Stocksbridge goal ace was unable to add another as the visitors ran out victors to claim the inaugural shield.

Top - On speaking terms. The teams line-up ahead of the It's OK to Talk Shield season-opener at Wombwell. Picture: Blue Line Photography.

Above - Apart from it all: A socially distanced view of the action at Wombwell.

Right - Yorkshire granite: A plaque marks the town's pride in Busby Babe Mark Jones.

2. IT'S SIMPLY SMASHING IN GOLDTHORPE

Thursday, August 13, 2020
Kingsmark Way, Goldthorpe
Dearne & District 6 Houghton Main 2
Friendly

It was a smash and grab raid that Goldthorpe old boy Alan Warboys would have been proud of. The prolific striker was picked up from schoolboy football in the village by Doncaster Rovers and went on to represent Rovers, Sheffield Wednesday, Cardiff City, Sheffield United, Fulham and Hull City but it was at Bristol Rovers he made his name. As part of the 'Smash and Grab' partnership with fellow Yorkshireman Bruce Bannister in 1973/4, they hit 40 goals to gain promotion, including an 8-2 demolition of Brian Clough's Brighton in a game featured on Match of the Day. In total Warboys scored more than 130 goals in about 500 League games during a 16-year professional career.

However, he was not the first Goldthorpe old boy to make his name for the Pirates. Wally McArthur joined Goldthorpe United from Denaby United and immediately attracted the interest of Rovers, who snapped him up in 1933. A 17-year career in the South West saw his notch 14 goals in 241 appearances in the distinctive blue and white quartered shirts before switching to a coaching role until he retired in 1962.

The latest generation of Goldthorpe players have a long way to go to match those records but have made a solid start to this year's pre-season campaign. They followed an 8-0 win over Doncaster Eagles earlier in the week with a 6-2 hammering of Sheffield & Hallamshire County League club Houghton Main's 'development' side. However, the game was much closer than the scoreline suggested, the difference being the superior finishing skills of the Doncaster Senior League side.

The day-glo orange-clad visitors certainly shone out but it was the home side who made the brightest start. Both teams struggled to establish control in the opening stages but it was the hosts who took the lead after 14 minutes when the impressive Luke Jackson picked up the ball from a half-cleared corner on the edge of the penalty area. With team mates bellowing for a pass left and right, the 19-year-old former Barnsley FC scholar glanced up and unleashed a superb 25-yard effort past the goalkeeper.

It was 2-0 five minutes later when a calamity in the away penalty area saw the goalkeeper and a defender collide in pursuit of a back pass, leaving No.9 Luke Vickers with a simple tap-in from barely six yards. The start of a conveyor belt of rolling substitutions for both sides spoiled the pattern but did give the visitors the chance to bolster their ranks and turn the tide. They halved the deficit after 28 minutes when a through ball found muscular Houghton No.10 Jamie Williams and he drew the goalkeeper before sending a delicious chip over his head to drop just below the crossbar, rippling all the way down the back of the net – don't you just love that sound!

With no linesmen, or corner flags for that matter, the over-worked referee called time two minutes early with the hosts 2-1 to the good and a closely-matched second half expected ahead.

The brief interval gave me chance to have a look round the tidy ground that Dearne moved into about four years ago, on the edge of a new housing estate, albeit the road junction being opposite the derelict and foreboding Goldthorpe Hotel. The smart ground is well looked after, well protected by a spiked fence and a large wall. There is loose hard standing round most of three sides of the pitch with grass behind the far goal, while the near side past the dug-outs is overgrown. A compact supporters shelter on the far side offers some cover, although most of the 120-or-so fans in attendance were within easy reach of the small 'Cross Bar' clubhouse. Inside the homely structure are some rustic benches with a separate room full of trophies, pennants and flags, showing the success of the club, which boasts a large number of teams, playing at several sites across the large village – providing football for more than 400 youngsters. The small bar boasts four pumps – bitter, two lagers and cider at £2.50 a pint – plus a fridge containing a selection of cans, with hot drinks and crisps, chocolate, etc, also available.

Suitably refreshed, it was back out for the second half and an unexpected avalanche of goals. Williams went close to equalising after 58 minutes when he stretched to reach a driven cross and sent the ball up and over the home keeper towards goal from an impossibly tight angle, Unfortunately for him, by the time the ball came down, a defender had managed to get back and scooped the ball off the line.

Straight up the other end and it was Dearne's turn to see an effort cleared off the goal line. That proved a short term let-off for the visitors though because within eight minutes they were 5-1 adrift. The goal of the game came from another of the hosts' youngsters on the hour mark. Eighteen-year-old right back Rowan Briscoe picked up the ball just inside the visitors' half and, after advancing a few strides, he fired a stunning shot into the top corner of the net from fully 30 yards.

It was all one-way traffic after that. Three minutes later Jackson sent a shot through a crowd of players from the edge of area. The goalkeeper was unsighted but did well to parry the ball but only along the goalline for Jamie Wootton to convert from a matter of inches. A short corner was played to Briscoe soon after and his deep cross was headed in by Jon Blessed to make it 5-1. Houghton pulled one back after 77 minutes when substitute Giorgio flicked in a free-kick but the scoreline was completed when Jackson added his second to bookend the result.

Goldthorpe is one of the most economically deprived areas of the UK and the club has faced an uphill battle to survive. Despite this, a superb community spirit exists. Three years ago, the club suffered a major blow when storage cabins at Kingsmark were broken into and £3,000 worth of grass cutting equipment was stolen. A spokesman said at the time: "We break our backs trying to keep this club running and then this happens. Devastated is not the word. And where do we go from here? We will have to raise more money to buy the things we already had, trying to again find the money. It makes me absolutely sick."

Within hours the community responded with local businesses putting out collection boxes and others, including schools, organising raffles, while mower businesses offered replacements at special rates. A year earlier, the community had raised almost £3,000 in a crowdfunding appeal to help towards the club's move to Kingsmark. As part of that £15,000 appeal, club chairman Antonio Jamasb took on the challenge of a six-day screwball rally, with his wife Sharon and three-year-old daughter Saffron. It entailed buying a car for no more than £750, getting into fancy dress and travelling around Europe without breaking down. They bought a 1995 Audi A80 with 170,000 miles on the clock and travelled to Strasbourg, via Koblenz, Prague and Hanover on a 2,280 mile journey.

'Bettina' only just completed the trip, thanks to advice from Facebook friends as the challenge would have been void had they called on the rescue services. The rally raised about £3,000 and Bettina now sits next to the Cross Bar at the ground.

Now the club is giving back to the community. They have been nominated for a Proud of Barnsley award in recognition of setting up a food bank during the coronavirus pandemic. They converted their new pavilion into a food bank in April. Chairman Mr Jamasb told the We Are Barnsley website: "We have always wanted our new pavilion to be a community hub. We were due to have a grand opening in March, which was cancelled due to the virus, and we began thinking of ways we could help our community. One of our members suggested that we use the pavilion to open a food bank and so we did a bit of fundraising and got started."

Now they organise collections and deliveries to many families throughout the area. "It's great that we have been recognised," said Mr Jamasb. "It's nice to know that people think of us. I have been trying to spread the message to the kids that you can't judge others by their appearances and that it doesn't take a lot to be kind. I am hoping that they will carry this message on for the rest of their lives. We never expected the food bank to go on as long as it has but it's great to feel like we are making a difference in the community."

Always looking for innovative ways to promote the club and district, Dearne & District have agreed a partnership with IFilmFootball. The company will be recording all the first team's Saturday matches at Kingsmark Way and streaming them via

YouTube. Club and player sponsors will be included on match and highlight videos on the dedicated channel.

Although Dearne & District FC are a relatively new club, formed in 1982, the history of football in Goldthorpe goes back much further. Goldthorpe Institute won the Montagu Cup in the early years of the 20th Century, with Goldthorpe United also successful in the 1920s. Goldthorpe Colliery played in the FA Cup in 1921, while Goldthorpe United chalked up 22 ties between 1928 and 1935, including wins over Maltby Main Colliery, Hatfield Main, Norton Woodseats, Hallam and Yorkshire Amateur, reaching the third qualifying round in 1930/1. Many of those ties were played at the Welfare Ground, which is still in use at the other end of the village, shared with the cricket club.

Above - Keeping an eye on the time: Action from Dearne & District's win against Dodworth. Left - Rallying round: Dearne's Screwball Rally entry.

3. MAIN GAINS

Saturday, August 22, 2020
Tickhill Square, Denaby Main
Denaby Main 1 Sutton Rovers 0
Friendly

It is 18 years since I last visited Tickhill Square and not a huge lot has changed. The ground still has the imposing miners welfare club behind one goal and the equally distinctive St Albans Catholic Church at the opposite end. The pitch has its remarkable side-to-side slope with the sturdy covered terrace at the top side – which replaced the 500-seat former Hellaby Greyhound Stadium grandstand that was demolished in 1992, having been shipped from near Rotherham 60 years-or-so earlier.

However, missing is the traditional old stand opposite and the floodlights, as well as my hosts on that day in May 2002 – Denaby United. In their place are Denaby Main JFC, who have made the ground their own with plenty of signage and a new changing room and tea-bar block at the alternatively named uPVC Trade Centre Ground.

A new United were formed in 2011 and now play in the Doncaster Rovers Saturday League, after briefly climbing the ranks to the Sheffield & Hallam County Senior League. They are based at the Old Road playing fields in the neighbouring village of Conisbrough. The original United were formed in 1895 as Denaby Parish Church and enjoyed a success-laden history, competing one level below the Football League in the Midland League for many decades. They reached the first round of the FA Cup three times and enjoyed a record crowd of 5,200 for the visit of Southport in 1927.

Even in their final years, the club enjoyed regional success with former professionals Mel Sterland and Imre Varadi helping them to the Northern Counties East League title in 1987. They were the last in a long line of players who either moved on to Football League sides or left the professional ranks to join the club, including a Manchester United transfer record holder and numerous top-flight stars and England internationals.

Among those who learned their trade at Denaby was England international Jack Barker. He earned 11 caps while playing for Derby County, who he joined for £200 from United after recovering from a thigh injury suffered in the pit.

Lionel Smith made also six appearances for England and won the FA Cup and Football League title during a 160-plus game career at Arsenal, having joined the Gunners on amateur forms from Denaby just before the Second World War.

Leslie Hofton joined Manchester United from Denaby in 1910 for a club record £1,000, beating the Red Devils' previous record of £700 – such figures are hard to believe compared to modern-day multi-million fees.

Wally Ardron, who went on to score more than 200 goals for Rotherham United and Nottingham Forest started life at Denaby and Reg Attwell was chosen for the Football League XI during his time with West Ham, Burnley and Bradford City, while Walter Aveyard averaged more than a goal every two games for Sheffield Wednesday and Birmingham City before moving on to Port Vale and Accrington Stanley.

George Briggs scored 100 goals in 300 games for Birmingham City, earning a call up as reserve to the England team but never gained a cap.

Sam Cowan was the only player to represent Manchester City in three FA Cup finals, captaining the team in the 1930s and earning three England caps.

In more recent times, Denaby old boy Chris Beaumont made a name for himself when he scored the winner for Chesterfield in their FA Cup quarter-final win against Wrexham in 1997.

Topping that was Cliff Parker, who scored twice for Portsmouth in their 1939 FA Cup final win over Wolverhampton Wanderers. He had started his career at Denaby and, after spells with Doncaster Rovers and Pompey, returned to see out his playing days at his old club.

Eddie Boot became a Huddersfield Town legend, appearing more than 300 times in the blue and white stripes between 1937 and 1952, going on to manage the Terriers for six years.

Keith Burkinshaw was working at Dodworth Colliery, while playing for Denaby United but made a big enough impression to be signed by Liverpool. He made just one appearance for the Anfield club before going on to a long career in the lower leagues with Workington and Scunthorpe but it was as a manager he made his name, more famously at Tottenham Hotspur from 1976-84.

Another player who launched a management career from Denaby was Bobby Saxton. After 400-plus Football League appearances with Derby County, Plymouth Argyle and Exeter City, Saxton sat in the hot seats at Exeter, Plymouth, Blackburn Rovers, York City and, as caretaker, Newcastle United.

Moving in the opposite direction, Walter Bennett joined Denaby in 1907 with two FA Cup winners medals and a Football League championship title to his name, as well as two England caps and, closer to the modern day, Stewart Evans had been a member of the Crazy Gang at Wimbledon, helping them all the way to the old First Division under Dave Bassett. He joined Denaby in time to help them secure the 1996/7 NCE title.

Ground grading issues meant promotion above the NCE was not achievable and the death knell for United came when landlords Denaby & Cadeby Miners Welfare Scheme ordered them out. That decision was heartbreaking for the club's support, which numbered almost 500 for their final game and, with no alternative venue to play at, the club folded. At the time, club secretary Barrie Dalby told me in a feature for the Yorkshire Post that he had watched them for more than 50 years and added: "It's a tragic day for the club and a sad one for the whole community. The worst part is it's been done by local people."

He said that all approaches for negotiation have been refused by the Tickhill Square landlords. One of the reasons given by them for their decision was the lack of opportunities offered by the club to the local community by the semi-professional team. The landlords said they wanted to offer more chances to the local community and a semi-professional club did not fulfil that criteria.

A new club was formed, Denaby Main, and almost two decades on, they are meeting that requirement, with a thriving youth section feeding into their adult side, which is preparing for a seventh season in the Sheffield & Hallamshire County Senior League after progressing from the Doncaster League, during which tenure they competed alongside United.

Any bad feeling about the circumstances of the demise of United and the rise of Main appears to have been papered over, if not buried completely, with the derby rivals having competed for the John Hurley Memorial Trophy in memory of a former United player.

But back to the present day and Tickhill Square still retains a buzz with many historic parts of the 100-year-old-plus stadium still visible, including terracing and crowd barriers, albeit much of it now overgrown. Unfortunately, the grand old stand was a victim of a fire and had to be demolished in about 2005. The entrance to the ground is in front of the brooding bulk of the miners welfare club, opposite gates emblazoned with Denaby & Cadeby Cricket Club's initials. There is plenty of car parking outside the entrance and in the welfare car park. The Welfare was a thriving social and sports club with a swimming bath and library, as well as the football and cricket grounds, plus social and entertainment rooms indoors, catering for the welfare of miners and their families for generations. The large red brick building, complete with stone crest and pillars, is now looking forlorn with the pits it served long since gone – Denaby Main Colliery in the late 1960s and Cadeby Colliery in 1986.

Tickhill Square still boasts hard standing all round the pitch but much of the metal surround is gone. New brick-built dugouts are in front of where the main stand used to be with three steps of the original terracing, complete with crowd barrier alongside. More work is planned over the next year. The large covered standing area opposite is five steps deep, next to the four-year old dressing rooms and tea bar – complete with comfy armchairs and a TV. Cans of beer are available at £1.50 for those who cannot wait for the after-match welfare hospitality, with tea, coffee or that football staple Bovril on offer for £1 (or just 50p for a small one!). However, the most popular item on the menu seemed to be the burgers, freshly cooked while you wait and a bargain at just £1.50 – £2 with cheese.

Today's visitors Sutton Rovers, from the Doncaster League, are in a similar position to their hosts, having moved into a new ground with a long history. Rovers, who had been sharing at Askern, are the new tenants this season at the Welfare Ground, former home of Hatfield Main.

Hatfield were formed in the 1920s and were one of the top teams in the Northern Counties East League during the 1990s but folded in 2012 after brief spells in the Central Midlands and Doncaster Leagues. The Welfare Ground has continued to be used, most recently by Dunscroft United.

Strong wind and occasionally showers meant the covered terrace offered shelter, although the referee was obviously prepared, he wore his coat throughout the match – with no assistants to share any perceived 'blame' from either side, perhaps he was ready for a quick getaway! A crowd of about 90 witnessed a game lacking much goalmouth action but with plenty of energy expended and a few heated tussles that on another day might well have brought some cards from the man in the middle.

The only noteworthy first-half incident came after 25 minutes when Denaby's No.6 Cameron Till belied his small stature with a crashing 30-yard free-kick that stung the goalkeeper's hands on its way to smacking off the cross bar.

Sutton should have taken the lead six minutes after the break when a through ball saw the home defence caught out by a speedy attacker. The goalkeeper was slow off his line but the shot when it came was well wide. Denaby came close to the opening goal after 66 minutes when Christian Baxby chipped the goalkeeper from what looked an impossible angle on the junction of the six-yard box and goalline. The ball floated across the frame of the goal before bouncing off the top of the bar at the opposite post. Fifteen minutes later Baxby was denied in bizarre fashion. He found space on the edge of area but his shot was parried by the goalkeeper. However the momentum of the shot saw the ball bounce down and under him and fly high into the air and off the bar before spinning crazily back towards goal where it was pounced on at the foot of the post by the grateful goalkeeper to complete a remarkable save. The winner eventually came six minutes from the end when a long throw caught the Sutton defence napping and Ryan Dean tapped in from the edge of the six-yard box.

Let's hope Tickhill Square can continue to provide a classic football venue for generations to come.

Before and after: Denaby's main stand in 2002 and, as it looks 19 years later. 2002 picture: www.groundtastic.co.uk

4. CODE BREAKERS

Tuesday, August 25, 2020
The Lee Johnston Signage Stadium, Glass Houghton,
Castleford
Glasshoughton Welfare 1 Pontefract Collieries 5
Bill Cook Memorial Trophy

Football has long struggled to gain a toe-hold in the rugby league heartland of the M62 corridor. Tonight's opponents Glasshoughton Welfare and Pontefract Collieries have doggedly stayed around to become the area's longest-surviving football clubs, with the latter enjoying the rarefied atmosphere of the North/West Division of the Northern Premier League – the fourth tier of non-League football – still well adrift of the heights reached by the area's rugby league clubs.

However, that has not always been the case and things could have been so different. The Great Split of 1895 saw the Northern Union break away from the Rugby Union, opening the door for association football to gain the upper hand across the north. The earliest roundball pioneers in the West Riding were from in and around Pontefract and Castleford and the towns enjoyed early success, culminating in Castleford Town making two applications for membership of the Football League.

In 1919 Town were on an equal footing with newly-formed Leeds United, meeting them in the Midland League (drawing 0-0 at home in front of 3,500 fans but losing 6-0 away with 5,000 in attendance). Leeds joined the Football League the following season and in 1921 Cas tried to join them.

The formation of the new Division Three North saw 28 clubs vying for 18 places but, frustratingly, Cas finished 19th. Even so they gained more votes than fellow applicants Rotherham Town (later United), Doncaster Rovers, Yorkshire Leaguers Wakefield City and Scunthorpe United. At the time, that seemed to be a loss to the Football League as Town had huge potential, demonstrated by a club record 7,000 crowd for their West Riding Senior Cup tie with Huddersfield Town that season.

A year later, the club applied again but received no votes and soon after vacated their Wheldon Road ground, handing it over to recently formed Castleford RL club, who moved from their Sandy Desert ground on their eventual way to Super League stardom. After hitting the heights of the Midland League, Town dropped into the Yorkshire League and by 1937, after playing at Castleford Sports Stadium, were no more. Their 30-plus year life, which has started in 1905 in the Leeds League, had been eventful, rising to the cusp of the Football League and chalking up an impressive 72 ties in the FA Cup, including latter stage appearances against Reading and Bradford (Park Avenue).

A separate club, Castleford & Allerton, also represented the town in the Yorkshire League in the 1920s, while teams from neighbouring Altofts and Fryston have also enjoyed a long history at similar levels but it is now Glasshoughton who lead the way.

Down the road at Pontefract, Collieries have a long history, with links back to the 1930s as Tanshelf Gems, morphing into Pontefract United, before merging with a junior club to gain their present name in 1958. The town boasted a Yorkshire League club in the shape of Pontefract Borough, who had a single season of membership in 1928/9, also enjoying a four-game run in the FA Cup. However, it is only since the arrival of Collieries into the semi-professional ranks in 1979, when they joined the Yorkshire League, that the town has gained attention in the footballing world. Recent seasons have seen Colls climbing the non-League ladder and they went into tonight's match two rungs higher than their hosts.

Their opponents were formed as Sunday League works team Anson Sports in 1964 but changed their name 10 years later at the invitation of Glasshoughton Colliery, coinciding with a move to their present Leeds Road home. The original colliery team had a brief taste of the 'high life' playing four FA Cup ties either side of the First World War. Welfare started their non-League life in the West Yorkshire League, progressing to the Northern Counties East League in 1985, yo-yoing between the divisions but claiming West Riding County Cup honours in 1994.

This was my first 'restricted' game of the season with a

coronavirus-limited crowd of 150 allowed. Rain and strong winds all day saw many other games called off but, with no Twitter updates from Glasshoughton, I assumed the game was going ahead; confirmed by the visitors who said no inspection was needed and the game was on. I arrived half an hour before kick-off to discover cars queuing out of the car park, which was jam-packed. 'Oh dear' I thought and quickly checked alternative fixtures – but not many had survived the weather, with a dash to Cudworth to see AFC Wakefield take on Guiseley u18s my only alternative.

I managed to park in a side street and was relieved to see the turnstile still open and only a small queue of fans waiting to sign in. After paying my fiver, signing in and getting a free spray of sanitiser after using the communal pen, I was in – and only No.62 on the list, so I need not have worried and the crowd ended up being just short of 'capacity'.

The club's pitch is part of the larger Glasshoughton Leisure Complex, which includes a cricket field, bowls greens a five-a-side arena and the Glasshoughton Centre, with all manner of activities going on inside, hence the busy car park. The ground has hard standing all the way round with two similar-sized stands offering protection from the elements – one has six steps of standing behind the Leeds Road goal, with the other all-seater on the far side. The pleasant, neat and tidy, tree-lined ground, is bedecked in the club's blue and white colour scheme. A tea bar offered drinks and confectionery and also contained a small selection of home and away programmes in one corner.

The visitors had won the previous two Bill Cook Memorial Trophy ties and were favourites to triumph again in the Junction 32 derby clash; their grounds are just two miles apart, separated by the M62. A vociferous ground of a dozen young Glasshoughton fans – the Glassy Massive – kept up a barrage of chanting throughout the game; occasionally humorous, regularly abusive but certainly entertaining. Strong winds and drizzle throughout the game and occasional torrential downpours meant the stands were well-tested, while the cosiness of the officials' changing room was well vetted with the referee and linesmen deciding to sit out the worst of the storm at the start of the second half, leaving both teams to await their belated arrival, while getting steadily soaked through.

The two-division gap between the neighbours was obvious from the start with Colls a class apart for most of the game, looking faster, fitter, stronger and more skilful. But there was no wonder when you looked at the pedigree of some of their players – the latest to boost their ranks is young centre back Jack Cawthorn, from York City. He joins the likes of former Barnsley and Burnley defender Jordan Barnett and Callum Walmsley, who is on loan from Barnsley. Another team-mate is much-travelled Scottish League Cup winner Ben Gordon, who numbers Leeds United, Chelsea, Tranmere Rovers, Yeovil Town, Scunthorpe United, Birmingham City and Colchester United among his former clubs, as well as a host of non-League sides, plus Kilmarnock, who he helped to victory over Celtic in 2012 to clinch silverware north of the border. The Bradford-born left-back also has 15 England caps to his name, at u16, u17 and u20 level.

Ponte were on the offensive from the start and took a third-minute lead when a shot ricocheted to leave the home goalkeeper wrong-footed and former Farsley Celtic and Altrincham hitman Damian Reeves converted from close range. It was 2-0 22 minutes later after Ponte had dominated the play without producing an end result. Reeves was denied by the goalkeeper but his shot rebounded and fell kindly for Gavin Rothery to strike home via a deflection. The visitors cruised into half-time two goals to the good but it could easily have been six

Five minutes into the second half and it was 3-0 when Rothery's corner was cleared off the line but Reeves was on hand to head it into the net.

"We lose every week," chanted the home fans… "You're nothing special," they added. They also began singing "We're never going to score" and it did look prophetic when Albert Ibrahimi found space to curl in a shot from 20 yards to make it 4-0 after 68 minutes. But two minutes later there was hope for the hosts when their big No.9 pulled one back on the break.

The four-goal gap was restored in the 65th minute when Rothery ran across the area before making an opening to fire a shot just inside the post. Three minutes after that Reeves was being congratulated on a hat-trick when his deft header across goal dropped neatly under the bar, but his celebrations were premature with the offside flag ruling out the strike.

It was then Glasshoughton's turn to show their potential as the pinned Colls inside their own half for a lengthy spell. They were unlucky to go unrewarded when their right winger's 20-yard shot was blocked and his follow-up effort crashed off the crossbar. Soon after the same player outpaced the visiting defence and his surging run ended with a shot that left the Ponte goalkeeper grasping thin air but the ball hit the far post. That was the last of the goalmouth action as a multitude of substitutions continued to spoil the game's pattern.

It was just left for the teams to go through the motions ahead of the visitors being handed the trophy, the first silverware of manager Andy Monkhouse's reign. The former Rotherham United, Hartlepool and Swindon midfielder took over after Craig Parry left, along with most of the squad, to go to Worksop Town. In their place, Monkhouse has recruited an exciting blend of young, up-and-coming talent and a few experienced old heads. On tonight's showing, they are in for a successful season.

Room for one more? Restricted entry at Glasshoughton.

Glass act: A view from the Glasshoughton dug-outs.

5. WAKEY, WAKEY... CAN THE SLEEPING GIANT BE ROUSED?

Saturday, August 29, 2020
Millennium Stadium, Featherstone
Wakefield AFC 1 Rossington Main 4
Friendly

They say rugby league is a game for tough men. Even so I was a little alarmed when the gateman approached me pointing a gun at my head, asking me to remove my cap. Gulp! They take dodgy apparel seriously here I thought.

Thankfully, the 'gun' was merely a thermometer and was being used as part of the coronavirus precautions ahead of Wakefield AFC's historic opening match in Featherstone.

Mention Featherstone to any Northerner and the one word associated with it, whether a rugby league fan or not, is Rovers. Football comes way down the list. However, if new kids on the block Wakefield AFC have their way, the Millennium Stadium in Post Office Road will be seen as a major stepping stone on the way to establishing the forgotten footballing city on the map. The ambitious one-year-old club have moved nearer to 'home' after starting life over the Barnsley border at Cudworth.

This might have been the first football match at the ground in its 112-year association with Rovers, but two of the stands have witnessed football before, including a memorable FA Cup tie against Chelsea only 16 years ago. Remarkably, they used to be the East and West Stands at Scarborough's Athletic Ground (McCain) Stadium and were moved to the West Riding in 2011 in a mammoth operation using a huge amount of volunteer labour and passionate fans' support. Fans bought the stands from the defunct club and erected them at the railway end of their ground, replacing terracing. As part of the deal, the rugby club carried out the demolition of the rest of the Scarborough stadium.

Featherstone chief executive Simon Riley said at the time: "It was as if the stands were designed to fit. It was like a giant

Meccano set. We numbered it piece by piece, moved it and put it back together."

Re-erected in Featherstone, one stand was rebuilt in its full form with the other being truncated, both now resplendent in Fev's blue and white. It was calculated that about 48,000 hours has been worked voluntarily on the stands by 'The Stand Gang' to help the ambitious vision become reality.

It was a promising start to life at Featherstone for their new tenants – an all-ticket sell-out crowd for their debut at the 9,850-capacity ground. Unfortunately, that capacity was limited to a paltry 150, due to coronavirus restrictions. Even so, all tickets were snapped up within 24 hours of going on sale earlier in the week for the first football match at the grandly named Millennium Stadium, Featherstone – not to be confused with the rather larger one that first appeared in Wales. This one is sponsored by a local learning disability business, Millennium Support Services.

Tickets were free with a donation bucket at the entrance point on match day. I arrived and, not surprisingly, found plenty of space in the car park. After my encounter with the 'gunman' as I approached the entry point, I had my ticket scanned before almost bumping into a tailor's dummy kitted out in the smart Wakefield home shirt – perhaps I needed the services of their sponsor – Eyewear Opticians!

Then came the first sign of familiarity – a man selling raffle tickets – and a food kiosk and bar. A bacon sarnie and cup of tea set me back £5.70 but the fare was popular with many fans scattered around benches set at the obligatory two-metre distance – including many obvious groundhoppers comparing notes.

Only the main stand is open for Wakefield games and a one-way system is in operation with fans seated well apart, equally spread across the three areas. There are seats around most of three sides of the ground with open terracing at the Post Office Road end and in the adjoining corners. The new goals sat in front of rugby posts but there was no sign of rugby league markings on the pitch and I could easily have been at a Football League ground.

The teams emerged from between stands on the opposite side of ground to a smattering of applause from a mainly 'neutral' crowd, with only the few visiting Rossington fans making their presence known vocally. Wakefield were in an all-white kit with Crystal Palace-style blue and red sash, while Rossington bore a strange shade of blue – think dark sky blue or faded navy.

Wakefield have been drafted straight into the Premier Division of the Sheffield & Hallamshire League, while Rossington ply their trade one level higher in Division One of the Northern Counties East League. The home team looked very professional during the warm-up. Their mainly young-looking team were in pristine kits, adorned with lots of sponsors and went through their routines meticulously. However, once the game started, it was obvious which was the higher-ranked team. Wakefield showed some promising touches with skilful individuals but Rossington's all-round team work soon gave them the upper hand and most of the first 45 minutes was played in the home half.

The visitors went ahead after seven minutes from the first corner of the game with centre back Alfred Thompson heading powerfully into the net to applause from the Rossington fans, with the shouts of players and management echoing around the ground. Wakefield enjoyed a short period of domination midway through the half when a Rossington defender lost the ball on the edge of his penalty area and No.9 Dan Palmer was clean through but goalkeeper Callum Fielding saved well. Two free-kicks in dangerous positions and a corner saw Wakefield push for the equaliser but they could not find a finishing touch and they paid the price, conceding a second goal after 24 minutes. A deep cross found centre forward Jack Watson and he juggled with the ball before setting up left-back Brad Billam to crash the ball home from close range. Rossington had dominated first-half play but it was home winger Bryce Orsini who had impressed with some tricky and skilful play.

Despite it being the August Bank Holiday weekend, the weather was bitterly cold, with strong wind and occasional drizzle – more like November – and the fans were relieved when the players eventually returned from the warmth of their changing rooms. Four minutes into the second half it was 3-0. A Rossington corner was headed away from goal but only to near the penalty spot where Watson scooped the ball in. The hosts were gifted a way back after 54 minutes when Orsini crossed from near the corner flag. It was a straight-forward catch for Fielding but he somehow managed to lose his grip and dropped the ball into his net.

The final goal came after 74 minutes when Jordan Buckham's free-kick squirmed from the grasp of Crescenzio Arvanitis and Tyla Bell reacted first to stab the ball over the line.

Wakefield AFC is the fulfilment of the 10-year dream of businessman Mike Hegarty. He told the Wakefield Express newspaper last March: "Wakefield is the UK's largest city without its own football team, something that football fans and proud citizens have complained of for decades. There's a huge demand for a professional club in Wakefield. After years of negotiations and a hunt for a suitable management team and guarantors we are able to launch Wakefield AFC with a clear plan to develop professional football in the city. We realise we have a long way to go to move the club up the league ladder, but we think we have most things in place."

The plan is to eventually share Belle Vue with the city's major sporting institution, Wakefield Trinity, but until then, the club have been playing wherever they can. The original plan was to share with Pontefract Collieries but that fell through and instead they started life in Cudworth before moving to Featherstone.

Kingpin for the new club is Chris Turner. The former Sheffield Wednesday and Manchester United goalkeeper is the club's director of football and Hegarty said: "It says a lot about our aspirations that we have Chris involved. He was a successful professional footballer and also a manager. I doubt that there's embryonic football club that has started with such a strong team. We are in an excellent position."

During the club's first season they became an accredited FA Charter Standard Adult Club and managed to develop their own academy. Hegarty said: "Our aim is to provide education in a multi-cultural environment that is safe and secure, while training and playing in a full-time football environment. Our relationships in professional football allow us to provide every opportunity for a player to progress to their optimal level in the game. Our model encourages our players to further their education, while playing football. We have a close relationship with Wakefield College, where we encourage eligible players to go to study BTECs, HNDs, HNCs, BAs and apprenticeships. Our players will gain recognised qualifications, alongside playing the sport they love. We also have accommodation for students, who originate from different parts of the country/world, who want to study and play with us.

"There are about 335,000 people living within the Wakefield District. While the area is known as a rugby league hotbed, it is clear that there are many people interested in and playing football as well as rugby league."

Alongside that community vision, plans are being laid to rapidly climb the footballing pyramid with a goal of achieving Football League status by 2033. The short-term aim is to be playing at Northern Premier League's Division One level by 2024. Football director Turner said: "It is a massive step forward for the club to enter into a partnership with Featherstone Rovers. I have to say how welcoming they have been towards ourselves. The training and playing facilities are first class. Our players, I am sure, will enjoy the professional surroundings and a top-class playing surface. This represents a major step forward in the club's history."

The first-team manager is former Doncaster Rovers and Yeovil Town player Adam Lockwood, who said: "We will be looking to help each other move forward to achieve where we both want to be; it's great to be part of another community club that has similar ambitions and will help all members of our club present and new."

Another club with ambitions to promote the city name is City of Wakefield FC, who were also formed last year and play in the Wakefield & District League. Founder Aidan Wells said: "The club has high aspirations for our future. In a decade's time, the club aims to be a Charter Standard Club with a well-developed academy structure. We intend to build year-on-year to establish a club known for good football and good times, establishing links with neighbouring clubs."

The club shares a ground at City of Wakefield Golf Club with Thornesians and St. Ignatius but did not enjoy a great start to competitive life in Division Two, losing all 15 of their league and cup fixtures when the season came to a premature end.

Defeats included 21-1 at Thornhill United plus nine other double-figure defeats with the best result being a 4-0 defeat at FC Broadway.

Wakefield AFC and City of Wakefield are the latest in a long line of clubs to try to break rugby league's stranglehold in the area. The predecessors are numerous and date all the way back to the 19th Century, jostling for prominence alongside Trinity who were formed in 1873. Trinity's Belle Vue ground has been well used by exponents of the round ball game. A Wakefield City club was formed in 1899, playing at Trinity's home in the Leeds League but they were expelled for non-payment of fines in 1902. Rob Grillo's excellent recent publication, A Noble Winter's Game, tracing the early years of football in the West Riding, also tells the tale of another 'City' club who began life in 1906, playing opposite Belle Vue at Elm Tree Street. They had lofty ambitions and entered the FA Cup in 1907 but a 13-0 defeat at home to Denaby United proved to be the death blow and they folded not long after.

Probably the most successful Wakefield City club appeared in 1920, playing at Coach Road, in Outwood, where their ground capacity was 8-10,000. They were professional from the start and were founder members the Yorkshire League with an average crowd of 1,500. Such was their impact that the Football League encouraged them to apply for membership when they formed regional Third Divisions in 1921, keen to get 'soccer' in the rugby league heartland. Dave Twydell's authoritative book about clubs who applied to join the Football League, Denied FC, tells the story in full. Despite the backing of the League, Wakefield City only achieved four votes. Undeterred, they stepped up to the Midland League but were soon found wanting and finished second from bottom, conceding 103 goals. They were now playing at Thornes Lane with plans to develop a 15-20,000 stadium but were soon back in the Yorkshire League, playing at Westgate Common. They managed just one win in their final two seasons in the Yorkshire League and folded in 1928.

Several other Wakefield clubs have come and gone in the years since, the most notable being the former Emley club. The Villagers found their hilltop ground unable to meet the criteria needed to step up the pyramid so they switched to Wakefield, sharing with Trinity at Belle Vue in 2000/1. A huge crowd for their Northern Premier League title-decider against Stalybridge encouraged officials of the desire for football in the city under the guise of Wakefield & Emley and Wakefield-Emley before it became Wakefield FC in 2006, coinciding with a move to Wakefield RU's College Grove ground. However, things fell flat and the club resigned from the league in 2014 with a view to moving back to Emley in the Northern Counties East League but wound things up soon after.

Another Wakefield FC made a fist of things in the West Yorkshire League, while Wakefield United attracted headlines when they pulled together a group of immigrants to represent the city. Now the city's footballing future lies in the hands of Wakefield AFC and City of Wakefield. Will either be able to change the course of history?

Blue is the colour: The former Scarborough stand at Featherstone.

Red is dead: The stand in its previous colours on the coast.

Terrace talk: Rossington on the attack against Wakefield.

6. A FIELD OF DREAMS

Tuesday, September 1, 2020
Sheerien Park, Ollerton Road, Athersley North
Athersley Rec 1 Charnock Richard 4
FA Cup, Extra Preliminary Round

They say that blood is thicker than water and when it comes to pulling together, not many clubs will be able to match the family spirit at Athersley Rec.

Formed in 1979, the club have lived a hand-to-mouth existence but continue to defy the odds at their smart Sheerien Park home. The Penguins were originally called Athersley North Juniors and among their ranks was Geoff Horsfield, who went on to greater things in the Premier League but never forgot his roots, donating £25,000 to his old club to help them gain FA funding towards ground improvements.

The club have progressed via the Barnsley Nelson League, Barnsley Junior League, Barnsley Association League and Sheffield & Hallamshire County League where, after lifting the title six times, they moved up to the Northern Counties East League in 2012. They were promoted to the Premier Division at the first attempt, despite, remarkably, not paying their players but actually charging them subs to play.

"It is all about loyalty, respect and being friends – these are the values we have built this club on," co-founder and club president Pete Goodlad told James Grayson, of Non-League Yorkshire. "What makes me proud is that we've gone through 5,600 players; I'm on my third generation with some of the families because their grandfathers played, their fathers played and now their sons are playing. It makes you proud because they are all friends. The club has won 98 trophies and my proudest moment trophy-wise was when we won the Sheffield Senior Cup when we beat Frickley at Hillsborough. People said we'd never win it because it was too big a competition for us. But that year, that side was unbelievable, considering we weren't paying."

Even more remarkable has been the transformation of Sheerien Park. The former Edward Sheerien School playing field was just an open field with one pitch, Goodlad told N-LY.

"The day we bought it we had to get 35 burnt-out cars off the field. The scrap man was rubbing his hands. The grass was also six foot high and a farmer baled it for us. We got the land off the council in 2003 and have done everything ourselves. We did get some funding and the main funder, who I can't thank enough was the Coalfields Regeneration Trust. We accessed quite a bit of money and that paid for the floodlights and stand, which was brilliant. The hardest part was securing the funding to secure the site. Before we could do anything with the land we needed a fence to stop people coming in. It took us six months to actually clear the site and it cost £77,000 to get the fencing up. People don't realise how much hard work has gone into the ground and it gets harder because there isn't as much money around as there used to be."

As well as Horsfield's donation, the latest crop of players also dug in, literally. "The lads all came to help out and we shifted 40 tonne of sand and 40 tonne of soil. They painted the fences. These were all fans, volunteers, footballers and managers from the club. We all did it together."

Goodlad is proud of Horsfield's progress and the values instilled in him during his time at Athersley. "He played in the Premier League and had a great life and career as a professional footballer. I'm really proud that we helped him on his way. It is a fantastic story. But we have had a few who have done alright – Dean Short, Jonathan Brown, Wayne Scargill, who played at Bradford; Gordy Owen. We've had some good-uns over the years."

Horsfield has fond memories of his upbringing and insists the style of play that served him so well was all learned at Athersley.

"I was a decent player at 11/12 and played for Barnsley Boys u12s. I lost my way a bit and my dad said I needed to toughen up," he told the UndrTheCosh podcast. "At 13 I was playing for Athersley alongside blokes who were 23/24, 10 years older than me and tough, hardened brickies, chippies and sparkies. When I went to my first training session I think my dad must have said 'just boot him, kick him'. After half-an-hour of that I wondered what was going on as I was being kicked from pillar to post. hen Dean Croft, one of the players who also went on to bigger things, said 'If you don't start kicking people back that's all they're ever going to do to you.

"I got back in there and 'boom' and that was my game plan all the way through the leagues after that," added Horsfield, who made a goalscoring Football League debut aged just 16 for Scarborough, later serving Halifax Town, Guiseley and Witton before joining Kevin Keegan's Fulham revolution. After that came goal-laden spells with Birmingham City, Wigan Athletic, West Brom and Leeds United, among others in a 400-plus game professional career that reaped about 120 goals with transfer fees in excess of £4 million.

Horsfield said he had promised Athersley that when he reached the Premier League and his wages went up, he would give them something back and so he donated £25,000 to help their ground improvements. "They've gone from strength to strength since then with a bar, floodlights and everything. I don't get up there as often as I should," he said.

One thing is guaranteed, he will receive a warm welcome on his old stomping ground and will still be treated as just one of the lads.

Repairs and maintenance are ongoing at Sheerien Park and Goodlad's latest project has involved a £10,000 GoFundMe appeal. "We don't have a rich chairman or benefactor so we have to patch things up and we beg, steal and borrow to do that," he told N-LY's Grayson. "We're a community club who run galas and bonfires for the community. We want to develop our own players and do things from within. That's what got us success over the years and we've got to a position no-one thought we would ever get to."

So far £3,321 has been raised towards the target and Goodlad said: "Athersley Rec FC have been at the heart of the community since 1979. We've laughed and cried together, shared success and failure. Now we need to come together once more. The Covid-19 outbreak has been devastating and we, as a club, face real uncertainty now and in the future. With monthly running costs and direct debits going out every day, the club needs people to pull together. Even the smallest of donations will go a long, long way."

Those efforts were boosted for the visit of Charnock Richard in the FA Cup, with a bumper crowd making the most of the recent relaxing of coronavirus restrictions, allowing a crowd of up to 300 to flock to Sheerien Park. Alas, there was no winning bonus to boost it further as the visitors ran out 4-1 victors, to the dismay of much of the 284 in attendance who had paid their fivers.

I pulled into the well-marshalled car park 40 minutes before kick-off and was greeted by an amiable gateman, who took my name and contact details before ushering me to the turnstile. A large crowd was building with a host of groundhoppers and photographers already in place, meaning programmes were already sold out. Determined not to disappoint, the club quickly ran off dozens of free team sheets and made sure they were distributed all round the ground.

A sunny evening ensured the club's bar was at maximum capacity with fans of both teams mingling happily and the food outlet was also doing a roaring trade – no menu just a choice of burger (£2.50), chips or a selection of hot drinks for £1.20. As the sun set, the ground and pitch looked immaculate in the day's diminishing glow – hard to believe it has once been a field full of scrap cars! The two main seated stands are behind each goal with two smaller standing ones alongside the entry point.

Sheerien Park has a mass of signage and advertising hoardings with the most impressive being the ground name spelled out in giant letters behind the far goal. The two standing enclosures contain signs paying homage to previous club legends with more signs around the ground offering inspiration for the next generation.

Hidden away behind one fence is a small shed, bearing a Shaw Lane club shop logo, the only sign of the ill-fated groundshare the club had with now defunct Shaw Lane, who soared to the NPL Premier Division before imploding. Dug outs are on the far side, which proved the most popular section of the ground with the touchline full of fans with beers in hand.

The floodlights are not the brightest and it was a struggle to read the visitors' shirt numbers. At first I thought they were numberless but close-up they had white numbers on their green shirts but blacked out so only a narrow strip of white was showing. It was a nightmare to work out who was who. No such problem with the home players, whose plain block numbers on their black and white striped kit was easily identifiable.

Charnock Richard are also relative newcomers to this level of the non-League pyramid, gaining promotion to the Premier Division of the North West Counties League in 2017, a year after joining the league from the West Lancashire League. Charnock is a small village more famous as a service area on the M6, north of Wigan, near Chorley.

The opening flurry of frenetic action saw tackles flying in and a handful of bookings from referee Philip Roberts were need to calm things down. Charnock gradually gained the upper hand and took a deserved lead after 27 minutes when Nathan Nickeas slotted in from the edge of the penalty area. The visitors took charge after that but it was all square when a cross was deftly headed home by Jimmy Pursell after 35 minutes as the hosts broke free. Teammates dashed across to congratulate the scorer, although one was damning in his faint praise: "It's a goal, but we're still playing f***ing sh**e," he blasted.

Athersley came more into the game in an evenly-matched second half but it was the visitors who earned progress thanks to their superior finishing skills. They regained the lead on the hour-mark when Carl Grimshaw's free-kick in the home 'D' crashed through the wall and bounced out of goalkeeper Aiden Tyas' hands. A mad scramble ensured with three efforts cleared off the line before Nickeas swooped to add his second. Daniel Regan had chance to wrap up the game three minutes later when he ran clear and drilled the ball past Tyas but pulled his shot wide.

The hosts were creating more chances but their final efforts were poor, blazed high and wide as they peppered cars over the wall behind the Charnock goal. They were made to pay when the visitors went 3-1 ahead after 69 minutes. A corner created panic in the Athersley box and the ball ping-ponged around the six-yard box before Lewis Haydock forced it over the line. After 75 minutes, Athersley sliced through the Charnock defence and substitute Alex Hutchinson crossed to find James Thompson well placed in front of goal. He took his time, controlled the ball, sent the goalkeeper sprawling but, alas, his delayed shot was blocked.

Athersley were so keen to get back into the game that in the second minute of stoppage time, when the ball was hacked over the fence for a throw-in near the corner flag, three balls were thrown on to ensure a swift resumption. Two more good chances went begging for the profligate hosts before Charnock confirmed a preliminary round meeting with Northwich Victoria four minutes into stoppage time when captain Grimshaw converted from the penalty spot.

That sparked a mass evacuation towards the exit, although the home fans were still in remarkably spirited mood, sharing jovial, if ribald, banter with the Charnock dug-out as they passed.

Packing 'em in: A big FA Cup crowd at Athersley after lockdown restrictions were relaxed.

Heading for goal: An aerial attack from Athersley.

7. LUCK OF THE DRAW PAYS OFF FOR LEAGUE NEW BOYS

Saturday, September 5, 2020
Brodsworth Miners Welfare, Woodlands
FC Doncaster GCT B 2 Denaby United 3
Doncaster Rovers Saturday League

Follow Yorkshire's newest non-League club and you could be in the money. FC Doncaster GCT are sponsored by Great Chief Tournaments, a company based in Holme-on-Spalding Moor, running competitions offering people the chance to win big prizes for the price of a raffle ticket.

"We offer great odds and aim to change people's lives for the better," they claim, with their website showing winners of all manner of prizes from cash to electrical goods and even cars.

The company is run by Allen Williamson and the new club feel like they've already won the lottery. Secretary Dave Garbutt said: "We knew Allen and he said we needed some help to get us started as a senior side. He has kindly offered that support to help us get the club up and running and tidying up the ground. He is brilliant and even got the diggers in to help us clear things up. Allen's main business is Allenesway Recycling but he runs the competitions as well to put something back into the community."

Although the club are a new name to the non-League scene, their ground is one of the county's oldest. FC Doncaster GCT are running two teams and playing at the former Brodsworth Welfare ground in Woodlands. That has been home to a variety of teams bearing the 'Broddy' title since 1912, with the latest incarnation, Brodsworth Main, having folded last season following a move to Doncaster Rovers' Keepmoat Stadium, and the earliest having won the Yorkshire League in 1925.

The new club came about when officials at Phoenix u18s decided they wanted to give their players an outlet into senior football. Garbutt explained: "We were running Phoenix from Sandall Park and played a few games at the Welfare. I'd been involved for about 10 years and we usually finished in the top two or three of the Doncaster Junior League and were Division One champions in 2018/19 but the players had nowhere to progress to. We wanted to integrate with Brodsworth for this season but they moved to the Keepmoat and then folded.

"That meant there was no senior team playing at the Welfare ground so I decided to speak to the trustees to see if we could start a new club there. They said yes and gave us a short lease, which is renewable."

So popular was the move to form the new club that the number of players soon exceeded the team places available. "We had the core of youngsters from last season's u18s and also brought in some players with experience of this league and the NCE," said Garbutt. "We were accepted into Division One of the Doncaster Rovers Saturday League but then a group of players who had been playing for Brodsworth last season asked if they could come back to the club. That would have meant we had too many players so they formed a second team – the B(rodsworth) team, and were accepted into the Premier Division. We are one club, but with two separate teams – the letter means nothing other than to differentiate between the two teams. It is purely the order they were formed, nothing to do with their standard."

That explains the confusion that has arisen in local football circles as to why the 'B' team is playing at a higher level than the 'A' team.

Garbutt said the club's short-term hopes were for both teams to gain promotion with plans already being laid to have a women's team and u17s in place for next season. Long-term the club hope to climb the pyramid to put the new club at least back at a level the former Brodsworth Miners Welfare team reached. That club was in the Premier Division of the Northern Counties East League only 10 years ago and enjoyed a bumper crowd of 1,251 in 2006 when FC United of Manchester visited in the FA Vase.

"The ground has been neglected for a few years and we wanted to bring it back to the condition it was in six or seven years ago," said Garbutt. "We've all been working hard, rebuilding walls, painting and generally tidying up, as well as bringing in bulldozers to get rid of a lot of the rubbish that had accumulated. We want to restore community pride in the Welfare and get the crowds back behind us to see that there is a successful team playing here. Today is the start of our journey and we've had to do it from a standing start due to Covid, etc."

By the time I arrived for the 'B' team match against Denaby United, the club had already made its debut with the Division One side having lost 2-1 to local rivals Adwick Park Foresters in a 12.30 kick-off to herald the start of a new era at the Welfare Ground.

My memories of Broddy were of a warm, friendly welcome, despite often grim surroundings, and the half-time pasties were gorgeous. I always seemed to miss the start of the second half just in case a fresh batch arrived! It was a familiar walk from the car parking at the Welfare club, alongside the cricket ground, where the club's second XI were enjoying an emphatic Pontefract League victory over Ryhill & Havercroft. The Welfare also has a bowls club, while next door is the village's impressive leisure centre. The entrance to the football ground used to be up a short, steep bank to a turnstile block but this is now derelict and, instead, admission is through gates at the bottom end of ground next to a snack bar building. The visiting officials room, where I so enjoyed those pasties, is no longer in use, although the club's new name adorns the outside, unlike the main entrance to the complex, which still bears the Brodsworth name.

A small covered terrace at the far end of ground looks to be a new addition since my last visit but the familiar old main stand on the halfway line, with its five rows of bench seating remains. The massive floodlight pylons dwarf those at the neighbouring leisure centre, with one set sharing a telecommunications tower.

About 60 people had gathered to see the latest team to call the Welfare home and the majority of them were home fans. They did not have much to cheer in a first half dominated by the yellow and blue-shirted visitors.

The hosts struggled to string passes together and regularly gave away the ball but somehow managed to turn around only two goals adrift. It took Denaby just five minutes to go ahead. Ashley Cantrill found space in the penalty area and curled a shot just inside the post. It should have been 2-0 seven minutes later when the home defence surrendered the ball just inside their own half, allowing Steve Ellis a clear run on goal. He advanced unchallenged to the edge of the penalty area but somehow managed to pull his shot wide as goalkeeper Lewis Gurnhill narrowed the angle. Aiden Oakley was then put through but snatched his shot straight at Gurnhill.

That was almost an expensive miss because FC Doncaster GCT carved out their first chance after 31 minutes when a free-kick from near the corner flag was met by the head of captain Hayden Tomlinson but the former Brodsworth and Askern player sent his glancing header across goal and wide. Steve Ellor doubled the Denaby advantage after 36 minutes. He shrugged off several challenges while twisting and turning to find space on the edge of the area before sending a superb shot into the far corner of the net with the outside of his foot.

The half-time break allowed me the chance visit the snack bar through a thick, chip-smelling smog. A small serving hatch was offering burgers for £2.50, chips for a pound (£1.50 as a buttie) but, alas, no pasties. I settled for a DIY tea. For £1 I was supplied with a cup of hot water and directed to a small table on which were tea bags. The snack bar bears plenty of reminders of the former hosts with Brodsworth FC press cuttings, pennants and a trophy cabinet, as well as redundant dressing room signs.

GCT emerged in their smart red and white striped-effect shirts and blue shorts for the second half and looked to be facing more of the same as they struggled to gain a foothold. No.9 Sam Kirk wasted a glorious chance when he was first to react to a cross but somehow contrived to miskick and sent the ball back over his own head away from goal. However, a triple substitution changed things dramatically.

The deficit was halved after 58 minutes when a corner was not cleared and fell to Kirk just inside the corner of the penalty area and he swept the ball into the far corner of the net to make up for his earlier miss. Three minutes later the game turned on its head. Tomlinson struggled to control a high bouncing ball 25 yards out but when it eventually fell favourably for him his shot proved too hot to handle for Denaby goalkeeper Dec Oxley and he could only help it on its way to goal via the far post. It became a much more even game after that with the home team now playing some quick-passing football to leave Denaby chasing shadows.

However, Denaby dug deep to stay in the game and were rewarded after 69 minutes when a corner created chaos in the home six-yard box. When the ball was only half cleared, centre back Dean Lucas, still up for the corner latched on to it and, with his back to goal, swivelled and sent the ball crashing left-footed across goal and into the net.

The last good chance of the game fell to Denaby three minutes later when a cross was deflected over his own goalkeeper by substitute John Brough but bounced off the bar and was cleared. GCT pushed hard for an equaliser but Denaby defended in numbers to see out the game and clinch all three points.

Former tenants: The gates reveal the previous club to have used the ground.

Old glories: The Brodsworth trophy cabinet remains in place.

Cornered: FC Doncaster GCT's Brodsworth Welfare home.

8. NO RAW DEAL
FOR PARKGATE

Saturday, September 19, 2020
Roundwood Sports Complex, Green Lane, Rawmarsh
Parkgate 4 Worsbrough Bridge Athletic 0
FA Vase, first qualifying round

Parkgate are Rotherham's highest-ranked non-League side but that has not always been the case. The area is a town suburb and got its name as the entry point to the 180-acre park of 18th-Century Wentworth Woodhouse country house.

After a brief spell in the national spotlight as the home of No.1 hitmakers Jive Bunny and the Music Factory Entertainment Group in the 1980s and 90s, nowadays it is better known for a large retail centre but has, in effect, become merely a part of Rawmarsh. Not so on the football field, where Parkgate's fortunes have obliterated those of its larger neighbour.

Until 1982 Rawmarsh Welfare had been the area's top side, winning six Yorkshire League divisional titles, including the overall championship in 1970; two Sheffield & Hallamshire Senior Cups and reaching the first round proper of the FA Cup in 1951. Add to that runs to the third round of the FA Amateur Cup, when crowds of up to 6,600 were attracted, and Rawmarsh made a decent name for themselves.

However, since they folded, when they were the only club not to transfer from the Yorkshire League to the Northern Counties East League when it was formed as a merger with the Midland League in 1982, it is Parkgate who have taken over the mantle of town top dogs. NCE runners-up in 2011, the Steelmen have also won the Division One title and the League Trophy, as well as reaching the final of the Sheffield & Hallamshire Senior Cup three times. Their popularity is growing and last year they attracted a record crowd of 1,536 to the Roundwood Sports Complex for the visit of Rotherham United, who use the facilities as their training ground.

It is not only the Millers who park their cars here though, there is also an 18-hole parkland golf course and bowls greens, all served by the towering clubhouse.

Parkgate's history is tightly linked to the neighbouring steelworks, which was founded in 1823. Other clubs have carried the Parkgate name but Parkgate & Rawmarsh United, Parkgate Works Sports and Parkgate Welfare did not stand the test of time, competing for attention with big brothers Rawmarsh, just up the road at the Hill 60 ground.

The present Parkgate club was formed in 1969, two years after British Steel was created, and represented the company's wire department. Their first manager was current chairman Albert Dudill. The Steelmen joined the Sheffield & Hallamshire County Senior League in 1970, gaining entry to the Yorkshire League in 1973 as BSC Parkgate. When British Steel was privatised, the club was renamed RES Parkgate in 1984 and has kept going despite several changes of company ownership, with the name changing to simple Parkgate in 1994. The latest company to take on the role of ground landlords are the Liberty Steel Group, who acquired the facilities in 2017 and set about reviving the steel works and leisure facilities, with the addition of the Rotherham United training facility adding extra kudos.

Parkgate's rise coincided with Rawmarsh's fall and the pair were in the Yorkshire League together for a bare eight seasons, although only in the same division for three. It was only in the final three seasons of Rawmarsh's life that they finished behind their neighbours in the standings.

Other than memories and a basic, rarely used football field, nothing remains of Rawmarsh Welfare. That is being challenged by former Rawmarsh Community School teacher Gary Cooper, who has written a book detailing the proud history of a club that boasted England World Cup winner Gordon Banks as one of its former players. The story of the rise and fall of Rawmarsh is told in the recently published "The Forgotten Heroes — the story of Rawmarsh Welfare".

It touches on the personalities and characters who turned out for Welfare at the sloping Hill 60 ground and was written after one of Cooper's pupils told him in a history lesson that his granddad had played for the club in the first round of the FA Cup. He started doing some research and the seeds for writing the book were born, as he told the Rotherham Advertiser.

"When I first considered writing, it was really just the FA Cup story," he said. "Then I discovered there was a bit more to it than that."

The near 200-page tribute draws on player interviews, documents and old newspaper cuttings and tells in detail not only the tale of how 'Banks of England' was rejected by the club as a teenager but also how star player Ralph Goacher turned down a contract at Manchester United because it would interfere with his new job at the steelworks. Things started to go wrong at Rawmarsh in 1970 with a news headline saying the club was £100 in the red and relying on bingo and cup runs to balance the books.

"The problems began in the 60s when vandals would get into the ground and knock walls down," author Cooper told the Advertiser. "There was a big fire as well and the social club was extensively damaged. The insurance premium hadn't been paid and there was no money to rebuild."

It meant that when the Northern Counties East League was created, Rawmarsh were not invited due to their sub-standard facilities.

What might have been had the club stuck with Banks long enough to earn a transfer fee for the talented world-beating goalkeeper? Banks' career started when he turned up in his pit clothes to watch local side Millspaugh Steelworks. The team's goalkeeper was not available and Banks was asked to play, despite having to do so in his work trousers, complete with coal dust. That display impressed Rawmarsh and he was asked to join them, despite being only 15.

His Rawmarsh career was short though, lasting only two matches. His first was a humiliating 12-3 defeat at Stocksbridge Works and when the team then lost 3-1 at home, he was told he wasn't good enough and released, rejoining Millspaugh. From there, he was picked up by Chesterfield scouts and went on to a star-studded career at the very highest level with Leicester City, Stoke City and England, before ending his career back in Yorkshire, playing for Scarborough as a guest in their 1976 Anglo-Italian Cup meeting with present-day Serie B side Monza.

Back to the present day and Parkgate are in FA Vase action, at the start of their 39th consecutive season in the Northern Counties East League. Opponents Worsbrough Bridge Athletic are another of only nine teams with continuous membership of the league since its 1982 formation. Can you name the other seven? Answers at the end of this chapter.

Despite the huge area of green, boasting its football pitches, golf course and bowling green, the Roundwood grounds are hard to find, tucked away in a maze of streets. A packed car park showed the popularity of the community complex and with lots of Rotherham United branding visible it was hard to spot where the longest-standing tenants play, although at least they do share the same team colours. However, a finger post in the top corner directs supporters to the turnstiles up the side of the imposing pavilion, which holds dressing rooms and the clubhouse.

Coronavirus precautions meant fans had to sanitise before entering the pay booth (£5 entry and £1.50 for the full colour, professionally printed programme) and once through the turnstiles, they had to submit contact details before being allowed in, after a "did you sanitise" check. You then turn right, past two small seated stands and a tuck bar behind the goal. There is a small covered stand, level with the penalty area and then three deep steps of terracing, high above the pitch and dug outs, with planking on the top step acting as a long bench. It means there are excellent viewing lines above the three-sided bowl with the vista stretching beyond the high hedge on the opposite side to the smoke and steam-masked steelworks.

A one-way system was in operation but, with only three sides of the ground available for spectators, it meant it was hard to negotiate due to it also being the viewing area. There is hard standing behind the far goal but no access to the touchline round that side.

The teams strode out on to an immaculate carpet-like pitch, led by the unusual sight of two female assistant referees – Danielle Knight and Clare Thompson – either side of referee Sam Clayton. The pair were far from overawed by the clash of the Steelmen and former Miners Welfare club, giving as good as they got when players questioned their decisions.

Parkgate manager Andy Dawson said in his programme notes that it had been the longest close-season he'd ever known – 28 weeks since their last competitive match, way back on March 7. Their next home match was scheduled for seven days later and, as luck would have it, the opponents were due to be Worsbrough again, this time in a league encounter.

Worsbrough kicked off in their all-blue away kit but that proved to be the only note-worthy incident of a half lacking in goalmouth action until almost half-time. The visitors relied on high balls up to their big No.10 Tom Foltyn-Brown, with the muscular man mountain dominant in the air but unable to carve out a clear chance. Parkgate, in their usual red and black kit, looked swift on the counter attack and finally made the breakthrough after 41 minutes. Tom Almond's deep cross from the near touchline saw home captain Bruno Holden hauled to the ground in the penalty area. Before the hosts could appeal for a penalty, the loose ball was rammed home by No.10 Freddy Tracey.

Worsbrough enjoyed their best spell immediately after the resumption for the second half and carved out a golden chance, failing to make a goalmouth scramble count.

Parkgate then stamped their authority on the game, doubling their lead after 55 minutes when a fantastic through ball from Richard Tootle released Tracey and his cross picked out Alex Rippon at the far post to stab the ball home. Holden then latched on to a goal kick from his own half and calmly swept the ball into the corner of the net. The scoring was completed in the 82nd minute when a scramble just inside the Worsbrough box ended with Rippon appearing to poke the ball into the visitors' net, but it was later credited as an own goal by Callum Turner.

Parkgate banked £550 for the win, witnessed by a crowd of 95, and booked a second qualifying round trip to Hallam on October 10.

* Of the 76 teams that played in the first Northern Counties East League season in 1982/3, only nine could boast continuous membership. They were: Hallam, Hall Road Rangers, Liversedge,

Maltby, Parkgate, Selby Town, Thackley, Worsbrough Bridge and Yorkshire Amateur. However, Liversedge and Yorkshire Amateur were promoted to the Northern Premier League for the 2021/22 season, leaving just seven.

Feminine touch: Women form the majority of the refereeing team.

Sign of the times: Restricted access to the stand at Parkgate.

9. HAPPY TO BE BACK IN THE STEEL CITY

Wednesday, September 23, 2020
Olivers Mount, Darnall
Handsworth 5 Athersley Rec 1
Northern Counties East League, Premier Division

Dr Who can't hold a light (or should that be a sonic screwdriver) to Handsworth FC when it comes to regenerations. The club has such a complicated history that it would pose a problem for even a team of Time Lords to understand!

It is story that goes all the way back to 1936 when Parramore Sports were founded as the works team of Sheffield iron-founders F Parramore & Sons. The company made stove grates, rain water gutters and sewer pipes, engineering castings, vices and clamps, as well as shells during the Second World War. The foundry closed in 1981. Parramore Sports was run by the works sports and social club and played in city works leagues at a ground near the Royal British Legion in Chapeltown and progressed to the Sheffield & Hallamshire County Senior League in 1985. In 2008 they joined the Central Midlands League, playing at the Don Valley Stadium, then changed their name to Sheffield Parramore, ahead of being promoted to the Northern Counties East League in 2011. The elevation brought a new ground with the club moving to Worksop Town's former Sandy Lane stadium and another name change, this time to Worksop Parramore and in 2011/12 they finished third in Division One to gain promotion to the Premier Division.

Meanwhile, another club, Handsworth FC, had been formed in 2003, playing in the Sheffield & Hallamshire County Senior League. They were promoted to Division One of the Northern Counties East League, winning the title in the 2011/12 season, finishing two places ahead of Worksop Parramore. However, ground grading issues meant they were unable to take their place in the Premier Division and, instead, were demoted back to the County Senior League. In the summer of 2014, just weeks after winning the County Senior League Premier Division title, that club merged with Worksop Parramore to form Handsworth Parramore.

The final name change came in June 2019, when the Parramore suffix was dropped, to become Handsworth FC and, this season, after an eight-year absence, the club returned to its Sheffield roots, at the refurbished Olivers Mount stadium, where Handsworth's reserve and youth teams had continued to play during their absence. Although the ground has had a complete makeover, including a state-of-the-art FIFA-category 3G artificial grass pitch, it remains short of the required standard for Northern Counties East League football. However, due to work being delayed by the coronavirus pandemic, special dispensation has been given for them to play there, while work is completed.

Vice-chairman Steve Holmes, speaking on the club's website, said: "We are absolutely delighted that the first team have been granted permission to move permanently back home to Olivers Mount."

He said the coronavirus pandemic had created many problems but their community-led redevelopment plans had continued, thanks to support from the Football Foundation, Football Stadia Improvement Fund and Sheffield City Council. "With the support of many local businesses and our hard-working and dedicated board of directors and trustees, we are proud to give our community and the city of Sheffield Step 5 football right in the heart of the Steel City."

He thanked the Northern Counties East League board for their help, guidance and understanding of the delays the club had suffered. "In conjunction with the NCEL board we came up with a matchday plan while developments continue that will enable Step 5 football to be played here," he explained.

Those plans have seen more than £1million invested in the project but work continues to finish building a new pitch-side facility, which will include home and away changing rooms, two officials changing rooms, a medical room, hospitality room, spectator toilets, matchday kitchen and pay booth.

Already in place are car parking areas and a licensed clubhouse, which houses a spacious bar area, four changing rooms, a medical room, a classroom/meeting room and spectator toilets plus, the jewel in the club's crown, a £700,000 FIFA-quality 3G pitch. Holmes added: "Throughout the lockdown the club chose not to reach out to the wider community for help for funding, etc, as we felt everyone had more than enough on their plate. "We have worked so hard to make this happen and appeal to our local community, to the wider footballing community in Sheffield and the surrounding areas to get behind the club. Get involved and make our home your home for non-League football."

As well as several football pitches, the site is also home to a cricket field, five-a-side pitch and borders Tinsley Park Golf Club. The new first-team pitch is a short throw-in from the A630 Sheffield Parkway and the whole site had been modelled on the set-up at Manchester City's Etihad Campus. The all-weather pitch allows the club to offer football to more than 500 children and the 3G surface means it is in use every day of the week.

Talking to the Sheffield Star last November, Holmes said: "We looked at how Man City set up for their junior, academy and scholar sides and basically we copied that. I wanted to make sure that the teams training on our pitch are getting the right set-up to help kids develop. It's fantastic to see it full every night of the week with different age groups playing out there."

Holmes is especially proud of the club's junior set-up, which has remained in the city during the first-team's absence, 15 miles away in Worksop. The most obvious success story is current Premier League top scorer Dominic Calvert-Lewin, the Everton striker, who played in the Handsworth youth section before joining Sheffield United.

He already has a place in the history books as one of only three adult England World Cup final scorers – Geoff Hurst and Martin Peters are the others. His claim to fame came in 2017 when he was part of the England team that won the u20 World Cup, scoring the only goal of the final. His colleagues included now-Everton teammate Jonjoe Kenny and four players who have gone on to play for the full England side, Fikayo Tomori, Lewis Cook, Ainsley Maitland-Niles and Dominic Solanke.

But for Calvert-Lewin's time at Handsworth, things could have been much different for him. He suffered from intense nerves and shyness as a child and told FourFourTwo magazine in December 2017: "Being nervous held me back. My dad took me to play for an under-sixes team and all the other kids were chasing the ball around.

"My dad said, 'Go on, get yourself off!' and I just jogged around on the outskirts not really wanting to get involved. I started crying and turned to my dad. He said, 'Come on, let's go.' A year later I joined the under-sevens at Handsworth and remember playing in a national tournament at Butlins, in Skegness. The first day we were there I was sick in the middle of the night because I was that nervous to play but I scored four the next day. I continued to score goals for Handsworth and was training one Saturday when a Sheffield United academy coach walked over. That was Scott Sellars and that was it. I signed for Sheffield United."

Calvert-Lewin was marked out for stardom at an early age. Chris Short was his assistant manager from u7 level at Handsworth and he told the Sheffield Star I'm June 2017: "Some of my best memories of Dominic were how he would put so much effort in to learn new things; how important it was for him to have a ball at his feet. He was football mad and a special talent. I remember a game where we were playing against Eckington at u7 level, and he scored four goals in 10 minutes. All were runs from his own half followed by a steady jog back to halfway line to start again. He was an amazing talent at a raw age."

Holmes is sure many more can follow the route carved out by Calvert-Lewin and he said: "As an established junior club, with pathways through to the first team, I don't think there's another club like us. We've had some great successes, not just Dominic. There should be a few more in the next few years and it's no coincidence there'll be more to replace them coming through."

With the first-team back playing alongside those youngsters, Holmes is keen to build on the opening night Covid-restricted gate of 247 to help the whole club progress.

"I'd love nothing more than to hear that turnstile clicking 400 or 500 times for every game. We're right on the gateway to the city. Our vision is a simple one... to become the club of choice for every aspiring young player and to continue to reward our community with great football... in their back yard.... at their club with the best possible facilities."

The club runs dozens of teams at all ages, for male and female, and continues to pile up the trophies and honours. Only last Sunday the club won cup finals at u7, u10 and u11 levels.

Handsworth's best attendance at Oliver's Mount was set in the 2011/12 season when 297 witnessed the Steel City derby against Hallam. Once the coronavirus restrictions are lifted, they could see crowds to match their club-record 1,561 for the visit of Sheffield United to their temporary home in Worksop for a friendly in 2016.

The visit of Athersley Rec for tonight's NCE Premier Division game was the first time the team had played at 'home' since April 28, 2012, when they lost 1-0 to Glasshoughton in front of 286 fans in a remarkable last week of the season. They then won their final game 2-0 at Worksop Parramore in a winner-takes-all NCE Division One title decider. The top three were all in direct competition that week and it ended with Handsworth pipping Glasshoughton to the title by three points with Parramore a further two points adrift.

Any fears the team might freeze on the big occasion this time were quickly dispelled as a confident first-half display saw them romp into a 4-0 lead. It took only six minutes for the amber and black stripes-clad hosts to take the lead when a defensive mistake allowed Marley Grant to nip in and slot the ball past Robbie Frostick in the Athersley goal. It was almost 2-0 seven minutes later when Leon Howarth sent a powerful drive narrowly over the bar. Strong drizzle built into a steady downpour but conditions underfoot remained excellent with the artificial surface responding well – less so the many unfortunate spectators who had not been able to find a socially-distanced place in the three stands and were without the protection of an umbrella.

Three young lads did manage to beat the elements, sheltering under a cover on one of the sets of goalposts around the pitch perimeter.

On the pitch, Athersley continued to face the full fury of the home storm and Frostick did well to keep out Sam Smith's 30-yard effort, which flew at him though a crowded penalty area, just managing to get across to paw the ball away. But Frostick was left helpless after 26 minutes when he failed to collect a long throw from the Popeye-armed right-back Sam Weston and Smith headed in. Two minutes later it was 3-0 when Bailey Hobson found space on the edge of the area and his deflected shot had enough power to leave Frostick wrong-footed. Howarth came close to scoring his second with a 20-yard curling effort that dropped just over the angle of post and bar before Smith wasted a golden chance, guiding a free header wide of the target with the goal gaping.

The first half scoring was completed seven minutes before the break with the goal of the game. Weston swung over a deep cross that looked to be going out of play but Smith somehow managed to hook it back across goal from a seemingly impossible angle and Howarth converted with aplomb.

Half-time brought the much appreciated announcement that Marie in the snack bar was serving steak pie, chips, peas and gravy with "Hendo's" – Sheffield's favourite relish! Whether the home players had indulged in a few too many pies, it was hard to tell but the second half was much more even with Athersley forcing the pace and unlucky not to score more than their one consolation goal.

The visitors' pressure was rewarded on the hour mark. Garside's 25-yard free-kick burst through the home wall to pull a good save out of Jordan Greaves. However, the half-cleared ball only went as far as the corner of the penalty area and the resultant cross was drilled home by Garside. That made it 4-1, but it could easily have been 4-4, had an earlier blitz of Athersley action been more rewarding. Handsworth tightened things up after that and the last action of the game saw home substitute Callum Walton tripped in the penalty area after a mazy run. He picked himself up to send Frostick the wrong way from the spot to complete the scoring in stoppage time.

For opening night, the only let-down was the weather but the restricted maximum of 300 meant only a few more fans could have been catered for had they decided to brave the elements. The hosts were superbly organised with many sanitising stations around the ground and entry points. Spectators had the option of 'signing in' electronically via a mobile phone scanning code or manually at the pay booth. Guidelines were listed in the programme, regularly updated over the makeshift public address system – run from the back of a van behind one of the goals – and club officials were friendly, welcoming and appreciative of the support they had attracted. The gate ladies, raffle seller and stewards were delighted to be 'back home' and their joy was evident for all to see. Admission was £5 with £1.50 for the programme.

The ground is obviously a work in progress but already looks to be something to be proud of with three stands along the 'top' side of the ground catering for seated and standing fans and hard standing round all four sides, including an elevated section alongside the stands. Once the changing room complex is finished and the snack bar and toilets duplicated nearer the pitch, it will be a magnificent stadium indeed. Special mention for the public address announcer – he could be heard clearly at all points of the ground, was easy to understand, and very informative, without being obstructive.

Rain later? A wet evening at Handsworth.

Brolly good show: A spectator provides his own shelter.

Group of five: Young fans stay within the latest social distancing advice.

10. HOLDING ALL
THE TRUMP CARDS

Saturday, September 26, 2020
Altofts Sports and Social Club, Lock Lane, Altofts
Altofts 3 Ripon City 3
West Yorkshire League, Division Two

When it comes to longevity, Altofts have clearly been playing their cards right. The West Yorkshire League side have been at their Lock Lane ground since 1894 and celebrated their 125th anniversary last year. Now languishing in Division Two of the league, they have an illustrious past and were among the first clubs formed in the heart of the West Riding.

It was further south that football got a toehold in the White Rose county with Sheffield being among the trailblazers in the 1850s. It took another 30 years before interest in football took off further up what is now the M1.

The first West Yorkshire Cup (later West Riding County FA Senior Cup) competition took place in 1897, with Hunslet winning for the first four seasons. Huddersfield were victorious in 1901 but then it was Altofts who took centre stage as the team from the mining village won it three times on the bounce, showing their strength ahead of the later domination of professional teams from Leeds, Bradford, Huddersfield and Halifax.

The reason Altofts were one of the first clubs to dominate county football was the fact that most of their players were drawn from the pit, with miners having been brought in from Staffordshire and the likes, where association football was already the no.1 sport. In this part of Yorkshire it was the oval ball game that was dominant; first union and then Northern Union (later rugby league).

With full-time clubs Leeds City, then Leeds United, Huddersfield Town and the two Bradford teams, City and Park Avenue, dominating the Senior Cup, a new competition was formed and again Altofts, now as Altofts West Riding Colliery, claimed top billing in the West Riding CFA County Cup. They were winners in 1920 with a team consisting of players who lived within a mile of the ground. Such was their strength they repeated the feat with the cup heading back to Lock Lane in 1924, 28, 29, 33 and 37.

Those achievements attracted national attention and a cigarette card company featured them on one of its collection. Yes, Altofts, were the Panini favourites of their day! An Altofts player also featured on another series of the cards in his own right. George Reed had started his career at Lock Lane before moving to Leeds United. The left-half went on to play almost 200 Football League matches for United, Plymouth, Crystal Palace and Orient between 1925 and 1935.

He was not alone; several other players moved from Altofts into the professional game as Football League teams mined a rich seam from this area of the Yorkshire coalfield. In fact the Altofts' alumni makes an impressive list.

It includes:

Jackie Deakin – centre forward at Bradford City, scored 45 goals in 62 games.

Keith Ripley – wing half at Leeds United, Norwich City, Mansfield Town, Peterborough United and Doncaster Rovers. Scored 45 goals in 320 games and was selected for the Football League against the Scottish League at Ibrox Park.

Bobby Webb – Leeds United, Walsall, Bradford City and Torquay United. 74 goals in 270 games.

Alf Whittingham – striker with Bradford City, Huddersfield Town and Halifax, 51 goal in 190-plus games plus 84 in 78 war-time games for Southampton, including eight in an 11-0 win over Luton Town in 1943.

Jimmy Glazzard – Huddersfield Town, Everton and Mansfield Town (152 goals in 324 games). Football League Division One top scorer in 1954, including a haul of four headed goals in Huddersfield's 8-2 win over Everton.

Others include: Eddie Dunn (Sunderland), Geoff Hartley (Rotherham United), Dennis Miles (Bradford Park Avenue) and Alan Parkinson (Bradford Park Avenue).

The next generation saw:

Terry Caldwell (Huddersfield Town, Leeds, Carlisle and Barrow).

Dave Fretwell (Bradford City and Wigan, as well as California Sunshine and Chicago Sting in the US League).

Ron Measham (Bolton Wanderers) and Dave Penney, the current York City director of football, who played at Derby County, Oxford United, Swansea City, Cardiff City and Doncaster Rovers. He has also managed Doncaster, Darlington, Oldham and Bristol Rovers

Skip to the present days and players with an Altofts' pedigree include:

Lee Crooks – 250 games for Manchester City, Northampton, Barnsley, Bradford City, Notts County and Rochdale before joining the RAF.

Chris Greenacre – 126 goals in 457 games for Manchester City, Cardiff City, Blackpool, Scarborough, Northampton, Mansfield Town, Stoke City and Tranmere Rovers before emigrating and playing for Wellington Phoenix, where he is now assistant manager.

Lee Brisco – Almost 200 games for Sheffield Wednesday, Manchester City, Burnley and Preston, plus four England under 21 caps – and Jamie Price – Leeds United, Doncaster, Halifax, Burton Albion, York City and Harrogate Town.

One player who did not move into the professional game was Jack Beddows. However, his legacy lives on. He was in Altofts' 1937 county cup-winning team and also played for the famous Pegasus FA Amateur Cup side, as well as the Combined Services during the Second World War. He served the club proudly for most of the 20th Century and the stand at the ground now bears his name.

Back to the beginning, and the club's early games were played behind the small colliery school at the top of Silkstone Row, the longest unbroken row of terraced houses in Europe. This ground proved to be too small, as the whole village would turn up to watch early friendly games. At that time, miners were paying a penny a week from their wages to play football and the colliery owners soon developed an interest and made donations. Most significantly, they helped the team move to Lock Lane, where the village cricket team was already in residence.

Gates of up to 3,000 were not unusual for cup-ties and such was the club's success in local circles and in the county cup that they elected to move up to the Yorkshire League in 1923, dropping out briefly for a championship-winning spell in the West Riding County Amateur League before returning to the countywide competition.

After the war, Altofts rejoined the West Yorkshire League, winning it at the first time of asking in 1947, and again in 1958, as well as adding the League Cup to their glittering trophy cabinet in 1952. Things changed in the 1960s with the colliery closing down and funding for the ground withdrawn. Lock Lane was handed over to Normanton Urban District Council (later Wakefield District Council). It meant tough times for the club, although they did still add to their silverware collection with successes in the Wakefield and Embleton Cups.

The West Yorkshire Premier League Cup was won in 1972 before a return to the County Amateur League brought the Division One title to Altofts in 1989. Success since then has been rare with their previous rivals having folded or moved up the league ladder. Instead the club has concentrated on developing young talent, not only for their own senior team but also as a launch pad for youngsters with much higher ambitions – as that list of players who have moved to the top of the game shows.

Among today's volunteers working hard to continue the good work done by previous generations at Lock Lane are treasurer Tim Lavin and reserve and u21 team manager Andy Newton. The pair were keen to talk about the excellent community work the club still does. Lavin said: "We've got teams from under-5s through to the first team and the new u21s bridges a gap to the seniors. We've also got a women's team. It's a really successful junior section and they have pitches all over the village, with two or three teams at most age groups. Eight u21 players were in the reserves in their last match so the pathway through the ages is really working."

Although the club is happy to give youngsters the chance to progress to as a high a level as their ability allows, the club itself is unlikely to push beyond its familiar West Yorkshire League surroundings. "Most of our players come from Altofts or Normanton, just down the road," said Newton. "We're strictly amateur and don't have the facilities to move up the leagues, even if we wanted to. Our derby games are against Rothwell. It used to be Woodhouse Hill but they closed their facilities. Snydale was also a tasty match but they're in the Premier Division of the Wakefield League now."

Today's match was definitely not a local derby with opponents Ripon City having to make a near 90-mile round trip for the fixture – an astronomical distance for this step of the non-League system. Remarkably, Altofts can claim only a four-year start on their opponents, with City having being formed in 1898 and playing at their current Mallorie Park ground since 1914.

One unusual sight at today's venue, so far down the footballing ladder, is that Altofts boast an impressive set of floodlights. That enabled them to field a team in the Northern u19 Alliance until fairly recent times, when opponents included much higher-ranked Bradford Park Avenue, the two Ossett teams, Frickley Athletic, Farsley Celtic and Guiseley. Success was enjoyed with a Central Division title triumph in 2011.

With no programme or team sheet for today's match, it was a case of asking referee Justin Sales to take a copy of his and he was happy to do so. In fact everything about the man in black was cheerful – he kept up a constant interaction with players from both teams throughout the match and the near-permanent smile on his face meant a problem-free but eventful encounter.

A strong wind, blowing in from the direction the M62 just a mighty goal kick away across a field from the other side of the cricket ground, made conditions not only difficult but also provided a constant drone of traffic noise.

The pitch has a barrier all the way round with the cricket ground behind one goal and a bowls green behind the stand. That has had to close due to coronavirus precautions, meaning the 60-or-so spectators had to huddle in their groups of six in any shelter they could find alongside the surrounding wall to keep out of the wind. Apart from some hard standing in front of the pavilion, the pitch has only a grass surround. Players and fans have to skirt their way round the cricket club nets, erected straight outside the clubhouse door, to reach the pitch, although the referee has an obstruction-free trip from his facilities in the car park-cum-all-weather training area. The pavilion clubhouse contains the team changing rooms, kitchen and bar, where the walls are adorned with old team pictures and an impressively-stocked trophy cabinet. Outside, a stone plaque high on a wall declares: "Altofts Athletic and Welfare Association funded by means of grants from the miners welfare fund 1922-26". The pavilion, although much added-to over the years, was state-of-the-art when it was built in the 1920s with hot and cold showers and baths (local villagers were still having to use tin baths in front of their open fire!). It also had a tearoom and was opened by Yorkshire and England cricketer Herbert Sutcliffe. At its peak, the ground also boasted a cycle and running track, as well as tennis courts.

Altofts were relegated to Division Two of the West Yorkshire League two years ago, having been promoted just 12 months earlier. They had earlier dropped into the bottom division for the first time in their history in 2015, having been in the Premier Division as recently as 2012 and having won the Division One title in 2009.

Opponents Ripon have been in the basement division since finishing bottom of Division One in 2016, after relegation from the Premier Division the previous season, following a recent high of fifth in the top division in 2013. Ripon had opened the new campaign with a 4-2 win at home to Swillington Saints, while Altofts went down 3-1 at local rivals Rothwell, so it was a good sign that I could expect some goals, and so it proved.

Altofts, in their usual red and black kit, held the upper hand after an early surge from the visitors against the wind and came close to scoring after eight minutes when left-back Chris Blankley's* 25-yard wind-assisted shot whistled narrowly over the bar. The visitors withstood that early barrage and took the lead after 17 minutes when a through ball found the tall No.8 Kyle Fox and he slotted the ball past home goalkeeper Harry Hardy. Joel Francis should have made it two after 26 minutes when he beat the offside trap and drew Hardy but scooped his shot wide. Ripon were made to pay for that miss two minutes later when James Playford crossed and Adam Swift's deft glancing header from near the penalty spot pulled the teams level. Swift was the only member of today's squad that had played in their Division One title-winning season, 11 years ago, finishing as top scorer with 16 goals.

Much of Altofts attacking play came from George Best-lookalike Playford with his tricky left-foot wing play providing plenty of entertainment. That threat was nullified in the second half when he showed his versatility by moving to right back. Jack Murphy's long free-kick drifted just over the bar for the hosts before the all-blue clad visitors regained the lead three minutes before the interval. Adam Haswell's cross-shot was kept out but the loose ball fell to Tom Coull at the far post and he tapped home.

Ripon danger man, the Freddie Flintoff-esque Fox saw a shot deflected narrowly wide before a quick counter-attack saw Charlie Taylor make it 2-2. A great run by Ripon substitute Gareth Barber saw him dash half the length of the field on a mazy run in the 76th minute before cutting in from the wing but Hardy was equal to the task, parrying his shot. Ripon went ahead for the third time with seven minutes to go when a neat through ball was dinked over the top of the home defence and Fox ignored the claims for offside to fire past Hardy for his second of the match. Altofts pushed forward to rescue a point and were rewarded in the 87th-minute when a deep free-kick found Oli Durkin at the far post to steer in another leveller past Ripon goalkeeper Louis Sutcliffe.

* Interestingly, Altofts' first West Riding Cup final team in 1899/1900 included Joe and James Blankley and the treble-winning team of 1902-04 also fielded a J Blankley. Today's line-up saw Chris Blankley at left back, a link between more than a century's worth of football in the village.

Play up! Altofts play their cards right.

No entry: The home enclosure is out of bounds.

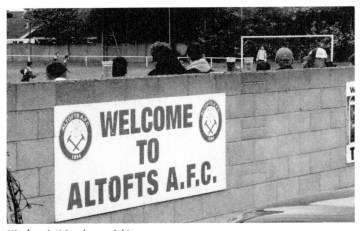

Mine's a pint! A welcome sight.

11. A CLUB WITH LEGENDARY STATUS?

Saturday, October 3, 2020
Coach Ground, Wakefield Road, Rothwell Haigh
Robin Hood Athletic 4 Boroughbridge 0
West Yorkshire League, Premier Division

The Sheriff of Nottingham has a lot to answer for... While his name has given Nottinghamshire the chance to lay claim to the legend of Robin Hood, it is Yorkshire that is the outlaw's rightful home. Robin Hood's Bay, on the North Yorkshire coast's claim to his name is a little spurious, but there is no doubt that the village of Robin Hood is in the mythical archer's real territory. Take your pick of where he was buried – Kirklees Priory, a dozen miles west, or South Kirkby church, a similar distance south east. His hunting grounds were around Barnsdale Forest, just to the east on the Great North Road (now the A1) in and around Wentbridge (venue for the meeting with Little John) and Campsall, where he married Maid Marian.

He even formed his own football team, with the diminutive Will Scarlett on the wing, Alan a'Dale orchestrating things in midfield, Much the Miller's Son at wing back, Friar Tuck between the posts, Little John at centre back and Robin himself arrowing in on goal from centre forward. The Merry Men, as they were soon nicknamed, in their all-Lincoln green strip, rattled up famous victories over the Guys of Gisbourne, Nottingham Sheriffs and King John's Park Rangers.

Okay, perhaps some parts of that tale might be a little fanciful... however, skip forward 650 years or so and the club continues to give to the community, albeit without robbing from the rich. The name first appeared in a map in the 1800s when a small community of homes was built for workers at Robin Hood Quarry in Rothwell Haigh. When coal was discovered nearby, the number of homes multiplied and it became a village in its own right. The football club was formed in 1952 when members of Robin Hood Youth

Club were looking to progress into senior football. They started playing as Robin Hood Youth Club A (it is not known whether that was an abbreviation for Adults or Athletic) in the Leeds Combination League, eventually amending their name to Robin Hood Athletic and moving to the West Yorkshire League.

Among their players in those early days was Roy Ellam, who went on to an lengthy career with Bradford City, Leeds United and Huddersfield Town before a spell in the USA with Philadelphia Atoms and Washington Diplomats, as well as short stints at the end of his career with Mossley and Gainsborough Trinity, where he was manager. He later ran the Nelson Inn, at Thornton Lees, before working at his daughter's fitness centre in Mirfield, eventually retiring to a West Yorkshire farm.

Robin Hood's honours include the West Yorkshire Premier Division Cup in 1976 and 1986, and four Leeds & District FA Senior Challenge Cups. They also won the West Yorkshire Division One title in 2014, after enduring a frustrating run of fourth, fourth, third, fourth, third and third-place finishes in the previous six seasons, when only two teams were promoted. The club have stayed at the top level of the Step 7 league since then and were joined last year by today's opponents Boroughbridge, who were also promoted as champions.

Situated on the A61, the main Leeds to Wakefield Road, Robin Hood boasts five pubs – the Rosebud, The Gardeners Arms, Halfway House, Angel Inn and Coach & Horses. It is behind the last of those that you will find the club's Coach Ground, previously a fallow field they took over in 1968 after originally playing at Sharp Lane. A stand was built in 1978 and remains today. The ground was bought by the club for community use in 2003 with a stipulation that it was always retained as a recreation space. Players used to change at the Coach & Horses but a substantial fundraising effort saw the club open new changing rooms, either side of the stand, as well as a tea room and store in 2011. Most of the work was completed by volunteers and took more than two years to complete. As part of the improvements, the 10-step terraced stand was refurbished, with solar panels added on the roof, providing not only energy for the club but also to be sold to the National Grid. The Andy Parker Stand now pays tribute to many of the club's benefactors, whose names are stencilled on boards on the back wall.

The Coach & Horses pub is currently seeking a new tenant but you can't miss the ground behind it, situated up a narrow lane off the car park, with a huge sign on the gate. There is plenty of car parking just inside the entrance as well as behind both goals. Apart from the stand and changing rooms/tea room complex, there are also dugouts, facing each other on opposite sides of the pitch. The club also boasts floodlight pylons in each corner of their ground but, bizarrely, they all face away from the pitch.

Team manager Matt Wright explained: "They face the training areas at both ends of the field, which for our level keeps costs down on a training facility. As manager I want us to push on to as high a level as possible but the club are happy as a strong Step 7 club and it would cost to go higher."

Steady drizzle all day meant only the bravest supporters ventured out but the pitch held up well, looking as good at the end as it did at the start. Praise to the groundsman! The crowd numbered about 25, all bar a few hardy souls in the stand, and another half-dozen-or-so venturing no further than their cars.

"We usually have a huge crowd but I'm guessing the weather was a deterrent," lamented Wright, who was frustrated to see such a small number of fans witness his side's first win of the season.

It was their third home game of campaign and they were still looking for a goal at the Coach Ground after a 0-0 draw with Headingley and an opening day 1-0 defeat to Beeston St Anthony. Victory had looked assured a week earlier at Hall Green United, but they squandered a 4-1 lead with 15 minutes to go and drew 4-4.

Boroughbridge has also made a slow start to the campaign; losing their opener 3-1 at home to Whitkirk Wanderers and following up with a 5-2 defeat at Beeston before gaining a 3-1 win over Huddersfield Amateur last week.

The confidence from breaking their duck was obvious with the all-blue kitted visitors making the early running and generally holding the upper hand in terms of possession and chances in the first half. However, it was the hosts who went into the break two goals to the good after defending stoutly and converting their chances.

Playing in red and black, Athletic withstood that early pressure and almost grabbed the lead after seven minutes. In a quick break, Matty Hamilton got in a shot from the edge of the area and a late challenge sent the ball looping up and over goalkeeper James Webster but he managed to recover to save beneath the bar.

The opening goal came after 29 minutes when Athletic broke away after defending two corners. James Finlayson saw his shot blocked but curled the rebound into the net. Two minutes later the visitors were left shell-shocked as they fell further behind. Joe Clulow delivered a pin-point cross to the far post where Hambleton powered home a header. Boroughbridge should have reduced the arrears six minutes before the break when a scramble saw a home defender handle the ball on the line. Referee Brandon Buckham awarded a penalty and booked the offender after consulting with a linesman. Chris Simpson stepped up for the kick but Lee Wood guessed correctly and dived low to his right to keep out the shot.

Half-time brought a dash to the tea room door – led by the visiting players, whose changing room was inside the same entrance door. A selection of hot drinks and refreshments was welcome and gave the chance for a quick look round the impressive facilities, adorned with team pictures, framed shirts, tributes to former members and a selection of trophies, as well as a television and dart board.

Despite their 2-0 lead, the home fans were nervous and one said: "We were three-up last week and blew it. They look a good team and there's still a long way to go."

After the interval, Boroughbridge again made the stronger start but, urged on by vocal assistant manager Liam Willingham, the home side dug in. Willingham's strong North London accent cut through the rain and mist with ease but seemed strangely out of place on a pitch dominated by West Riding and North Yorkshire brogues.

Aroused from any half-time torpor, Athletic responded to the encouragement – whether they could understand it or not! – and came close to a third goal. Hambleton ran through on goal and the slipped the ball across for Clulow but goalkeeper Webster blocked his shot well and the ball bounced up on to the bar and down on to the line before being cleared.

"It was just like 1966," said manager Wright after the game. "It hit the line but unfortunately our assistant referee said it had not crossed."

It was no great loss though because after 51 minutes a through ball saw substitute Mark Atkinson and Bridge goalkeeper Webster in a 50-50 race for the ball. The home player won and the ball fell for stand-in captain Chris Coupe to slam it home. Ethan Thorpe was the most outstanding player for the visitors with his tricky and skilful play seeing him pulling strings in midfield and he came close to scoring with a 30-yard effort that curled narrowly wide. Athletic's Lee Bennett was unlucky to see a 20-yard shot sail just over the bar but was guilty of an atrocious miss soon after when a defender gifted him the ball on the edge of the area. With the goal gaping, he blazed high and wide. Boroughbridge continued to play their part in an entertaining game but when they closed in on goal they were unable to take their chances with the home defence, well marshalled by debutee Jake Tonkinson, showing a never-say-die attitude, throwing themselves at any danger. Substitute Mark Atkinson set up the final goal after 80 minutes when he charged down the left wing before cutting in and delivering the ball on a plate for Clulow to tap home at the far post. The visitors had further chances to get a consolation but Simpson's shot from 20 yards was an easy save for Wood and Phil Wix also failed to test the home goalkeeper soon after.

In the final minute, Athletic substitute Alfie Hill set up Hambleton with an open goal but he steered the ball wide under pressure from Webster. After two minutes of stoppage time, referee Buckham brought proceedings to a halt and sparked a race for shelter from the continuing downpour.

Four goals, a missed penalty and plenty of entertainment, despite the weather – and all with no admission charge. Robin Hood continues to stand and deliver!

Railing view: Robin Hood's stand is well framed.

Taking cover: Fans watch from under shelter at Robin Hood.

12. A WOODLAND WONDERLAND

Saturday, October 10, 2020
The Stafflex Arena, Storthes Hall Park, Kirkburton
Shelley 6 Wyke Wanderers 2
West Yorkshire League, Division One

If you go down to the woods today… you're sure of a big surprise – quite a few in fact! Good sat nav and a keen sense of direction are needed to find the ground, but it is well worth the effort and it had not stopped the go-ahead club soaring up the league ladder.

Shelley's tidy Stafflex Arena is tucked away up a track in Boothroyd Woods, which is found up a narrow country lane, off a half-hidden turn on the opposite side of the A629 from the village. However, things have taken a turn for the worst recently and today's encounter gave Shelley the chance to end a miserable period in their long club history and halt their losing start to the new season with six of the best.

Today's adversaries had managed just three goals between them in their five games so far this season – so eight in just 90 minutes was amazing. That was nothing compared to the shock suffered by Shelley earlier in the season. All ready to start their third campaign in the North West Counties League and aiming to build on last year's curtailed season, when they were sitting joint second in the table after 31 matches, just ahead of county neighbours Emley and Golcar, they suffered a devastating bombshell.

With two pre-season warm-up matches already under their belts plus a club-first FA Cup appearance, as well as a delayed League Cup semi-final, they found the rug pulled from under their feet by the coronavirus pandemic. Proud to not only call themselves a community club but actually include it in their official title, the club decided it was for the greater good to pull their first team out of the semi-professional league and concentrate on their amateur and junior teams. A statement from the club, issued on September 18, included: "It is with real regret and disappointment that Shelley Community FC has withdrawn from the North West Counties League. As a result of the very challenging and uncertain economic climate caused by the coronavirus pandemic, the club is to revert to all-amateur status Most of the major income streams have dried up, making it impossible to cover the projected operating deficit going forward."

That saw the majority of manager Ash Berry's squad depart, including the scorer of their final semi-professional goal, Sam Awty, to Northern Premier League side Pontefract Collieries. He had netted in September 5th's League Cup defeat at Northwich. Barely a month later and only captain Adam Daffern and vice-captain Oliver Ghee remained at the club, with Berry having to completely rebuild his team for their return to West Yorkshire League action after a two-season absence. Daffern had also been in the Shelley side that last played in the county competition in 2017/18, before they gained elevation to Step 6 of the non-League pyramid.

The club had enjoyed a long and successful career in the Huddersfield League, rattling up a shed-load of honours since first being formed in 1903. But after lifting divisional titles six times, the Groom Cup three times and a Dearne Valley League and Cup double for good measure, they decided to step up a level and joined the West Yorkshire League nine years ago.

The original club had folded in 1972 but was reformed eight years later by current manager Berry, Paul Hirst and Steven Shephard and, in 2000 moved to Skelmanthorpe Rec. The club grew and, with the support of the Leslie Sports Foundation and the Football Foundation, moved to Storthes Hall in 2011 where, after several years of hard work, the facility was formally opened by Sarah, Duchess of York in June 2015. Originally the sports ground for Storthes Hall psychiatric hospital, the ground was used as a training base by Huddersfield Town before Shelley took up residence.

Success in the West Yorkshire League was instant as the team steamrolled their way to the Division Two title, rattling in an impressive 144 goals, winning 26 of their 30 league fixtures. Of that squad, Gino Dignan, Liam Berry and 38-goal Andrew Farrell were on today's team sheet. It was more of the same the following season with 21 more goals from Farrell helping gain second place in Division One to secure a place at the top level. They enjoyed five seasons in the Premier Division before moving west of the Pennines to test their mettle at semi-professional level. After a season of acclimatising, the club were enjoying a promotion charge until coronavirus reared its ugly head.

Now they are playing two steps lower down the ladder, taking the place of their reserves in Division One of the West Yorkshire League, who ironically, had been nailed on title winners until Covid 19 hit. Shelley has been due to be playing at Bootle in the second qualifying round of the FA Vase today, instead they were battling to secure their first points of the West Yorkshire League campaign. They were taking time to re-establish themselves at the lower level and sat rooted to the bottom of the standings going into today's match, after suffering defeats in their opening two games – 2-1 at home to Salts and 3-0 at Otley Town. That was after their first two scheduled matches – at G&C Hartshead and Featherstone Colliery were postponed to allow them time to pull things together.

Wyke, meanwhile, had a full set of results after four games – an opening day 2-1 win at Oxenhope Rec, a home 2-0 defeat to Pool and a 0-0 draw at East End Park with a postponement last week at home to Kirk Deighton Rangers.

The legacy of Shelley's short stint at level 10 of the football pyramid is a terrific ground. On a hillside surrounded on three sides by trees, it has stunning views across to Emley Moor and the iconic masts on the fourth. All the facilities are on one side, on top of a bank, making the most of the stunning vista but situated level with one half of the pitch, giving a slightly lopsided appearance to things. The quaint clubhouse building houses a cafe, and changing rooms with nine deep steps of terracing and seats down the bank, with two areas under cover. Dug-outs are at the foot of the bank with three sides of the pitch consisting of slabbed hard standing and grass on the far one. It is one of several pitches at the University of Huddersfield site, which hosts four senior and 20-plus junior teams, as well as Huddersfield Town Ladies.

However, despite their large membership and number of clubs at all age levels, the first team were attracting crowds averaging only around 50 for their North West Counties League matches; the biggest being 115 for the visit of country rivals Steeton – although they did attract 225 when Penistone Church arrived in their first FA Vase tie in 2018. Barely 20 spectators were in attendance today but they witnessed a classic on the immaculately prepared surface.

The club won the Sheffield & Hallamshire Grounds Team of the Year award in 2018 and 2019, capping that with national victory in the Step 5 and 6 awards. Unsurprisingly, club founder and first team manager Berry is also involved in that side of things, working with Stuart Crank and Rob Hardy. "It's a fantastic advert for our club and for grassroots football," said a club spokesman, who added: "Thank you to our grounds team and to every volunteer who had given their time to help make our grounds the best it can be."

Community is key to the club and the sports facility and football club are owned by the Leslie Sports Foundation, a registered charity. All income, sponsorship, subscriptions and donations that the club receives are reinvested into the club, with the charity being focused on raising additional monies to cover the shortfall, and to maintain the facility for the use of the wider community. The Buena Vista cafe at the ground provides community groups with access to an events and meetings facility and is dementia-friendly, with a permanent Sporting Memories Box used to support people affected. The foundation is also committed to developing disability football and runs weekly after-school clubs at three schools for young people with special needs in the Kirklees area. The club also run u12 and u16 pan-disability teams that are affiliated to the FA's Ability Counts League, as well as the open-age Shelley Creative Minds Team, who compete in the FA's Good Mood and Ability Counts Leagues.

Visitors Wyke Wanderers, from the Brighouse side of Bradford, are also proud of their community roots and the 51-year-old club, boast several senior and junior teams, playing not only at several sites in their home village but also in neighbouring Scholes. They offer a pathway through from the junior level to senior football, demonstrated today by the inclusion of 16-year-old goalkeeper

Matty Leaper. The youngster had an eventful game, saving an early penalty but then being beaten by a deceptive free-kick.

An exciting end-to-end start to the match saw both teams determined to end their recent poor spell. Eight minutes in and Shelley had a great chance to open the scoring but were unable to add the finishing touch to a mad scramble in the visitors' goal area. Straight up the other end and a good chance was wasted with a forward blazing high and wide after running unopposed into the penalty area. They made up for that with the opening goal after 22 minutes when a cross was floated in and the home defence was slow to deal with it, allowing Wyke captain Joe Hebblewhite the chance to stab in the loose ball.

That lead lasted only three minutes with Rickardo Ianzitto crossing for home captain Deffern to head in from eight yards.

The hosts had a great chance to take the lead after 27 minutes when referee Ian Thornton spotted a handball and signalled for a penalty. Long-serving Dignan stepped up but his effort was too close to Leaper and the youngster dived to his right to push the shot away. He had little time to rest on his laurels though because from the next attack he was left grounded. A high ball into the Wyke box saw him flap at the ball under pressure from the onrushing strikers and was left claiming he had been elbowed on the side of the head, as the ball was hacked clear.

A period of Wyke pressure was ended after 33 minutes when Shelley broke away and Oliver Sutcliffe shot down the wing before crossing for Kieron Taylor to convert from close range. Wake came close to making it 2-2 just before the break. There seemed no danger when a high ball was pumped in from the wing but, with no strikers near, right-back Daniel Hallitt stuck out a leg and diverted the ball over his own goalkeeper, but thankfully for him, also clear of the bar.

The two sides retreated for the interval, with Wyke staying out on the pitch, while their opponents sought the sanctuary of their dressing room. Both sides were keen to turn their chances into goals after an often feisty first half that had seen the two captains called together by referee Thornton to calm down their, at-times, over exuberant teammates.

Wyke made a stronger start to the second half and almost levelled in the opening minute when left back Martyn Hall got on the end of a free-kick and fired a shot towards the back of the net, only for home goalkeeper Stuart Morrison to pull off a stunning stop to send the ball on to the bar and away to safety. Wyke's young custodian was left red-faced after 63 minutes when Ghee's free-kick from near the touchline floated over him and into the top corner of the net. Refreshingly, the Wyke defenders were quick to encourage, rather than berate him.

It was 4-1 after 71 minutes when Taylor crossed from the goalline and strike partner Sutcliffe powered home a header from close range. Shelley extended their lead to four goals after 79 minutes when Ghee delivered a tantalising cross for Daffern to stoop and head in his second goal of the game. That became 6-1 a minute later when a scramble ended with substitute Thomas Brooke hammering home the loose ball from near the penalty spot.

Wyke book-ended the scoring in the last minute; having claimed the opening goal, they also netted the last one, when the referee spotted a misdemeanour and pointed to the spot for the second time at that end of the pitch. Wyke substitute Etienne Levis stepped up to send Morrison the wrong way to complete the eight-goal feast.

Long-distance call: Fans exchange pleasantries at Shelley.

Twin towers: Emley Moor's TV masts on the horizon.

13. KINGS OF THE CASTLE GOING TOP OF THE CLASS

Saturday, October 17, 2020
Earls Orchard, Slee Gill, Richmond
Richmond Town Reserves 1 Hawes United 1
Wensleydale Creamery League

It has been named as the most scenic football ground in England and groundhoppers from across the UK and beyond have made a pilgrimage to the beautiful Yorkshire Dales home of Richmond Town at Earls Orchard. Situated next to the glorious River Swale it sits beneath the imposing battlements of the town's Norman castle.

Unfortunately it is that history and magnificent setting that is stopping the club from progressing further up football's hierarchy. Restrictions on developments mean the club are all set to move into a new home at Richmond School as they aim to climb up to the Northern League.

Scenic as it is, the ground is decidedly basic and for today's fixture the pavilion was only partly open with many players arriving in their playing gear or changing in their cars, with their kit bags strewn along the touchline and in front of the shuttered pavilion – its opening ribbon cut in 1975 by then-Middlesbrough manager Jack Charlton. A post and rail barrier separates the pitch from the grassed spectating area with another fence between the ground and the neighbouring Coast to Coast footpath and the roaring Swale beyond. On the other side, the ground rises sharply with sheep dotted on the hillside above cottages overlooking the tranquil scene.

Referee John Dunwoody arrived just 15 minutes before kick-off but already changed for action. A quick chat revealed that he had rushed across country, having refereed a match in the Yorkshire Christian League in York. "It's got a lot of teams with ex-offenders in and I had to show a red card," he explained, adding: "Hopefully there won't be any more here."

He was almost right. Although the players escaped with only a handful of bookings between them, one member of the visiting coaching staff was dismissed for overdoing his protests.

Richmond's reserves normally play their home matches elsewhere in town and Dunwoody double-checked that it was indeed the second string in action at the iconic venue, even though he lives just the other side of the river. Dunwoody also revealed a family connection to the hosts. "My son used to play for Richmond but has moved to Bedale now," he said, adding proudly "He got a championship medal when he was at Oxford United and has been playing for Nicosia in Cyprus. He's in the Army so is limited as to how high a level he can play."

A player from so high in the footballing world playing at this level might seem unusual on the face of it but not so at Richmond. The first team are managed by Neil Tarrant, who numbers Aston Villa, Ayr United, Darlington and York City among his former clubs. However, he made his name in the Scottish League, claiming the Division Three Player of the Year Award for Ross County in 1999, when he scored 25 goals, bettered nationally only by Celtic's Henrik Larsson. The much-travelled Darlington-based striker, who is still signed on as a player at Richmond, has also played in Ireland, South Korea and Norway during a 15-year career that wound down with a handful of clubs in the Northern League before taking over at Earls Orchard. He played five times for the Scotland u21 team, thanks to a Macduff-born grandmother, and also holds the record for the highest transfer fee received in the Scottish Third Division at a reported £250,000 from a move to Aston Villa, where he had the No.14 shirt in a squad that included Gareth Southgate, Ugo Ehiogu, Gareth Barry, Paul Merson, Dion Dublin, David James and Benito Carbone.

Alongside Tarrant in the first team dug-out is the equally experienced Alan White, who mustered more than 600 games and 40-plus goals in a 22-year career that included spells at Colchester United, Luton Town, Darlington, Leyton Orient and Notts County. Their current on-field ranks include Leyburn-born Liam Darvill, who enjoyed a short professional career 10 years ago, coming through the youth ranks at Leeds United before loan spells at Rotherham United and Tranmere Rovers. He also played for York

City and Harrogate Town in the National League and picked up 10 England caps at u16 and u17 levels with honours including the Victory Shield. He was also named in the England u18 squad alongside Danny Rose and Danny Welbeck.

In the other direction, one player who started his career at Richmond Town before moving on to greater things was John Peverell. He went to Darlington via Ferryhill Athletic and rattled up almost 500 appearances for the Feethams club between 1961 and 1972, earning himself a place in the club's all-time best 'Dream Team'.

Bob Ledger, though, is probably the club's best-known former player. He played for Huddersfield under Bill Shankly, when Denis Law and Ray Wilson were his teammates. He also played for Oldham, Barrow and Mansfield, where he was in the team that beat West Ham in the FA Cup when they had a legendary line-up that included World Cup winners Bobby Moore, Geoff Hurst and Martin Peters. "Big Bob" made his name as a no-nonsense striker but was also known to play on the wing, in midfield and defence when needed and also appeared between the sticks as emergency cover.

His Huddersfield career ran from 1955 until 1962 and he went on to record a Football League tally of 60 goals in 360 games. He left professional football and played amateur football for Lancaster Town, Gateshead and Stockton, while working as a road builder and scaffolder, before moving to Richmond Town, where he spent the rest of the 1970s and some of the 80s. He had played in the area prior to that though, carrying out his National Service at Catterick, alongside Peter Swan of Sheffield Wednesday, Jimmy Melia of Liverpool, and Manchester United 'Busby Babes' Eddie Colman and Duncan Edwards.

The route to Richmond from the A1 still goes through the massive army camp – the home of the British Army in the North – with lots of military signs and notices, vehicles and squaddies bringing a slightly surreal scene ahead of what lies just along the road in beautiful Richmond. When full, Catterick Garrison is one of North Yorkshire's largest towns – boasting a population of about 25,000 – only Harrogate, Scarborough and Selby are bigger. The man responsible for siting the garrison where it is was Robert Baden-Powell, founder of the Scout movement, who was stationed at Richmond Castle.

The castle was built in 1071, following the Norman Conquest, and it is now the best-preserved early Norman castle in England. According to legend, King Arthur and his knights are sleeping in a cave underneath the castle. Apparently, they were once discovered by a potter named Thompson, who ran away when they began to wake. Another legend tells of a drummer boy who got lost while investigating a tunnel, and that his ghostly drumming is sometimes heard around the castle.

Now it is Richmond Town drumming up support as they switch from their ground beneath the mighty walls to one higher up the town at Richmond School. As well as the restrictions on development at the ground, car parking is also tight and another reason the club is keen to make the move. One disgruntled neighbour allegedly took exception to being barred from exercising his dog on the pitch and apparently calls the police if anyone parks on the kerb. However, it is only on match days, and he doesn't call on bank holidays when the roadside is heaving with tourists.

But that will not be a problem for much longer with the move to a new ground imminent. Not that they will be escaping the wrath of their neighbours. Objections to plans for development at the new ground have included: "By building a clubhouse you increase the likelihood of children hanging around it on a night. This will be an attraction for children from nearby estates, increasing the risk of crime, litter and noise.

The floodlights will be too bright and dazzle for miles around. Horses on a nearby bridleway would buck their riders on to the pitch. There will be an increase in anti-social behaviour with the risk of cheering, shouting and fighting spilling out into the neighbouring area."

Thankfully for the club, those fears were appeased and their plans have been accepted and work in now complete on The Clark Arena. It is named after the deputy head teacher at the school, Dave Clark, who was killed by cattle while walking his dog in a field last month.

First team manager Tarrant was a spectator at the reserves' Wensleydale League meeting with Hawes because his side's scheduled Wearside League game at Wolviston had been called off due to a waterlogged pitch. That helped boost the crowd at Earls Orchard with several first teamers and club officials enjoying the chance to sample extra action on the ground, with about 40 spectators inside the ground perimeter plus dozens more passing by and taking time to sample the action from the long distance footpath.

Tarrant was somewhat surprised by the objections to the new ground and said: "I can't say we have much of problem with Ultras at the moment! The new ground is ready; we're just waiting for FA approval. All being well we'll be able to start there on November 1. We've got one more home game here before then, although we will be keeping this pitch for use by other teams at the club. The new ground has a 4G pitch and all the facilities we need to move up the Pyramid. We're restricted here because we can't build, due to restrictions on the site because of its history and protected status.

It is disappointing to be leaving this ground but we need better facilities. A few of the more senior lads have grown up on the pitch and don't fancy the idea of playing on plastic at all but we need to move to progress. All we have here are changing rooms and a kitchen with a small tuck shop on first-team match days; there's no chance of having floodlights or anything like that. The new ground has everything in place – a grandstand, floodlights, 4G pitch, our own pavilion with a function room and really good facilities for both us, as the main tenant, and the school, whose land it is on.

"One of our players, "Uchie" Uchenna Anyadiegwu, is head boy at the school and he was part of the school's fundraising team who came up with the idea of naming the ground after the teacher. We've also had funding from the Football Foundation and Richmondshire Council were keen to support it as it is the only council area in the county without a suitable all-weather facility.

"The Clark Arena will be up to Step 5 and 6 standard, meaning we could go all the way up to Division One of the Northern

League – or Northern Counties East or North West Counties League, depending on where the FA send us – when we are in position to step up."

The present ground has a long sporting history and Peter Wicks, a club volunteer and former publicity officer, said: "Before becoming a football pitch, the ground was used by a local racehorse trainer to exercise his horses. His stables were in York Square, a stone's throw from the ground. Going back further still, it was used as a jousting ground. The joist holes, which supported the balcony from where the earl and his court watched the knights of old jousting on the green, can still be seen when you look up at the castle from the side of the pitch. We are keeping the present ground on in some form – whether it is for use by the reserves and veterans' teams or divided up into smaller pitches for the juniors, hasn't yet been decided. We've got 21 teams at the club covering all ages, up to veterans, as well as a ladies team, and most will be able to be catered for at the new ground. At the moment they play all over the area.

"The club have played here for about 90 years, under a variety of names – Richmond FC after the Second World War, Young Conservatives and Camerons United in the 1960s and now Richmond Town. We get lots of groundhoppers coming from all over Europe because of 'that' view. Unfortunately that is also the reason we have to move as it is holding us back but we will be very sad to leave. We had been playing in the Wensleydale League but moved up to the Teesside League. After we won a trophy quadruple in 2012 – the league title, Lou Moor Trophy, Macmillan Bowl and North Riding County FA Saturday Cup, we were elected into the Wearside League but with the ground as we have it, that is as high as we can go."

Earls Orchard was voted England's most scenic football ground in an on-line poll run by FC Non-League Football, a company that films non-League games. It beat three other finalists, Matlock Town, Esh Winning and Fisher, polling almost 40 per cent of the votes. To add to that honour, the club's home was also elected as the most beautiful ground in the Ridings by the Yorkshire Independent FA last year.

However, back to today's match and after securing the team sheets from referee Dunwoody, it showed to be a truly family affair with Richmond fielding three sets of brothers, including twins, and Hawes two.

It was the hosts who made all the early running and they held the upper hand for most of the game but failed to create many clear-cut chances and needed a stoppage time goal to salvage a point. The first chance fell to the hosts after seven minutes when a scramble in the Hawes six-yard box ended with Richmond's No.9, Owen Kelly, on his debut, firing a shot across the face. Hawes created only two notable chances in the opening half with the first seeing Daniel Barningham breaking clear after 15 minutes but his 20-yard shot drew a comfortable save from Mark Walker. Another home player making his debut was Brandon Bishop and he sent a 30-yarder fizzing narrowly over the angle of bar and post after 26 minutes. The visitors took the lead after 40 minutes when a free-kick just outside penalty area hit the wall but the rebound fell kindly for Thomas Wallis to slam in.

The teams cancelled each out for much of the second half but Richmond began to dominate and James Kelly blasted the ball past Guy but it slammed against the bar and bounced down just in front of the goalline before being hacked clear by a relieved defender. More pressure followed and Town's man of the match, 17-year-old Anyadiegwu, tried his luck with a delicate chip towards goal but Guy parried the ball.

The equaliser finally came in the second of seven minutes added on when a deep cross was flicked home by substitute Gary Walker, his header sneaking just inside the angle and out of the reach of Guy to spark relieved celebrations from the hosts.

Home fortress: The towering walls of Richmond Castle.

Feeling sheepish? Another view of the picturesque Richmond ground.

14. MAKING THE NEST OF THINGS

Tuesday, November 3, 2020
Miners Welfare Ground, Rotherham Road, Swallownest
Swallownest 1 Retford 2
Northern Counties East League, Division One

When it comes to 'pub teams', Swallownest are unique. This is no tale of Sunday cloggers, or an insult to their comfortable facilities, no it's a simple fact – Swallownest are the original pub team. However, rather than the club being named after a pub, it's the whole village that took on the moniker.

Named after the Swallow Nest hostelry, a wayside inn between Sheffield and Rotherham, the village spring up around it and took on its name in the 19th Century. Its growth was accelerated with miners moving into the area, working at Beighton, Brookhouse, Treeton and Waleswood pits, as well as the later infamous Orgreave.

Formed in 2006 as Aston, the club actually claims a longer heritage, back to 1959, when the ground's original tenants, Swallownest Miners Welfare, were in FA Amateur Cup action, a season before joining Division Two of the Yorkshire League. After a season adjusting to the countywide competition, they gained promotion, finishing third to Bridlington Trinity and Doncaster United. Two seasons followed in Division One, competing against teams including current Football League side Harrogate Town, Stocksbridge, Farsley Celtic, Ossett Albion and Bridlington Town, as well as the reserve teams of Scarborough and Goole Town. Five terms back in Division Two preceded a single season in the top flight. A 14th of 14 finish in Division Two in 1970/1 spelled the end for the club at that level, although they did continue to compete in the FA Amateur Cup until the competition ended, playing for two seasons in its replacement FA Vase, losing both ties before scratching from the 1976/7 competition. During their 14 years in the Amateur Cup, the furthest they reached was the fourth qualifying round, in 1961/2, although they did claim the scalps of Guiseley and Lincoln United in other seasons.

The present club started life in the South Yorkshire Amateur League, winning the league title in their second season. That brought elevation to the Sheffield & Hallamshire County League and two swift promotions saw them competing in the Premier Division in 2010, when they changed name to Swallownest Miners Welfare. Success was immediate with the club clinching the league title. The Miners Welfare suffix was dropped in 2016 and a second league title in 2017 saw them promoted to the Northern Counties East League after significant improvements to their Rotherham Road facilities, which had lost much of its previous infrastructure and by then consisted of a roped-off pitch, with remnants of terracing and pitchside fencing.

The ground now meets the necessary criteria, despite its unusual two-and-a-half sided appearance. Entry is off Rotherham Road, hidden up a track with a sign hidden behind overgrowth and access to the car parks along a weed-strewn drive. Thankfully the floodlights were on to offer guidance to the sports and social club (members only during the pandemic), behind which the ground sits. Most facilities are behind the near goal at the entrance to the ground. Land behind the far goal is out of bounds with a fence and a row of trees masking the immense backdrop behind – across to the twinkling bright lights of Sheffield, with occasional fireworks trails adding to the nightscape. Two small stands are behind the nearside goal – one with four deep levels of benching, the other standing only. These are separated by the entrance building, tea bar and changing rooms entrance. Another small seated stand is on the dug-out side. These sit alongside two gazebos, offering additional cover for the coaching staff but there is no entry for fans beyond the halfway line.

The club offered online admission, with the £5 entry fee paid a day before and the match ticket allowing swift entrance and a warm, friendly welcome from club officials keen to ensure everyone followed coronavirus precautions. With a programme just £1 and chicken pie and chips on offer for £3.50 it is a cheap night out. The food was plentiful and soothed my tea-less hunger pangs, with the pie filling still volcanic even after a walk to the far end of the ground. For fans, neither side of the pitch is particularly close to the action, with enough room between the touchline and barriers for a couple of small-sided pitches or perhaps space to turn the pitch 90 degrees should any future expansion plans demand it.

Anyone hoping for a pre-lockdown bonanza on the pitch were left disappointed with a scrappy game ensuing, although Retford fans could take solace in two late goals that earned them the points. In truth, that was the first time the visitors showed much attacking flair, with the hosts dominating possession. However, they could not build on a stunning early goal with smart interpassing moves frequently ruined by a final ball that could have been modelled on Peter Kay's "No Nonsense – 'ave it" John Smith's advert.

Rain throughout the day had made the surface tricky and with the clouds parting to reveal a near full moon, conditions were not the best for either playing or spectating as the cold gnawed at the bones.

Despite the campaign being barely six weeks old, the encounter had a real end-of-season feel to it, with the new lockdown ensuring at least another month of inactivity. It had started so well with Swallownest taking a third-minute lead when Alex Lill curled an exquisite free-kick arcing into the top corner of Retford goalkeeper John Kennedy's net. But that was it for the first half – not another single noteworthy incident.

A flurry of action warmed up the evening 10 minutes after the break. Luke Adby saw a shot cleared off the line but straight from the clearance the hosts suffered similar frustration when their effort was blocked by a defender with Kennedy grounded. A minute later the Retford goalkeeper flapped at a corner and gave Tyler Bradley an unexpected free header on goal at the far post but his downward effort lacked direction and bounced wide. The game then returned to a midfield battle until the closing stages when the heat was turned up.

With Retford belatedly pushing forward for an equaliser, they won a corner, which found its way to the far post where Adby headed in from close range, despite home claims the ball had not crossed the line – the linesman's signal said otherwise, demonstrating it was a good three feet over. Determined not to let their long-term lead have been in vain, Swallownest pushed forward for the winner but it left Evans exposed and a swift inter-passing attack for the visitors left the home defensive ranks depleted and Adby was left unmarked to slam the ball into the net to complete an unexpected turnaround with his second goal.

So that was my 149th different Yorkshire ground – when No.150 will materialise can only be imagined...

Lighting-up time: Illuminations at Swallownest.

Stars on show: Swallownest's Miners Welfare ground.

15. SALTS OF THE EARTH

Saturday, December 19, 2020
Salts Sports Association, Victoria Road, Saltaire
Salts 1 Pool 0
West Yorkshire League, Division One

Keen, Ryan, Warren, Cavanagh, McClum, Alexander, Barraclough, Boote, Clarkson, Rhodes, Stewart… won 1-0, Harry Warren scored t'winner in 10th minute. Hmm, it doesn't quite have the same ring to it as the legendary line-up of Haggerty F, Haggerty R, Tomkins, Noble, Carrick, Dobson, Dewhurst, Crapper, McIntyre, Treadmore, Davitt, does it?

Then again, I'm not Michael Palin and the team on show is Salts 2020 and not the heroes of a century earlier – Barnstoneworth United, as depicted in the famous 1979 Ripping Yarns tale of Golden Gordon.

The 1-0 result, also doesn't have the same resonance as "eight-one, eight-bloody-one", as memorably expressed by Gordon Ottershaw (Palin) before wrecking the home he shared with his wife (Gwen Taylor) and their son, named Barnstoneworth United Ottershaw.

Forty-six days since seeing my last live action, and 41 years on from that TV classic, memories remain strong in the minds of supporters and club officials at Salts. That is where the filming took place and where Gordon memorably got together the 1920s legends to see off Denley Moor 8-1 in a Yorkshire Cup tie, a week after losing by the same score to Brighouse.

Long-standing fan and former reserve team manager Vinny Gott joined the club two years after that seismic event in Salts' history and admits that, even though no-one is around at the club from those days, "Barnstoneworth" and "eight-bloody-one" are still commonly heard around the ground from fans and visitors alike. "We've all seen the programme and even now try to catch glimpses of bits of the ground we recognise – even though much of it is changed," said Gott.

Palin certainly left a lasting legacy and has kept the club in a list of 'must-visit grounds' for hoppers of a certain vintage. "When you watch reruns of that episode, you get the occasional glimpse of the corner of the old changing rooms and also the stands when they were both along the same pitch," said Gott."

Since those halcyon days, the club's Hirst Lane venue has been renovated with two pitches now lying head to head with a stand each and a four-team changing room block and tea bar that was built about seven years ago, along with an address change to Victoria Road (the grounds hasn't moved, it's just midway between the two roads and access is now easier from the Saltaire side). Just like Barnstoneworth, Salts can also look back on a glittering history – there's being in the 1950s – when crowds of more than 2,000 were the norm. The club was named as one of the top 10 amateur sides in the country after twice reaching the last 16 of the FA Amateur Cup and maintaining an incredible local league and cup record throughout the decade.

Nowadays, Salts ply their trade in Division One of the West Yorkshire League in front of two-figure gates, with ambitions no higher than a return to the Premier Division. Formed from the earlier Saltaire Mills club, Salts (Saltaire) began in 1924 and soon fielded teams in the Bradford Amateur and Bradford Industrial Leagues. They gained elevation to the West Riding County Amateur League before the Second World War and, in 1939, reached the West Riding County FA County Cup final, losing to Bradford Rovers. A league and cup double was enjoyed in 1946/7 and a string of district cups was soon added to the trophy cabinet.

Those stirring days saw neighbours Bradford City on the prowl and key players Arnie Kendall and Roy Brook were lured into the professional game. By 1950/51 Salts had regenerated with Don Glover leading the line. The prolific scorer rewrote the record books and, according to Ronnie Wharton's excellent The Best of Bradford Amateur Football book, hit five goals in a game three times and a double hat-trick against Yeadon in a 9-2 away victory. He then went one better, notching seven against Silk Street Labour Club in a 12-0 county cup romp. By the Christmas of 1950 he had found the net 49 times, including a hat-trick or more in five consecutive games. Silverware continued to pile up throughout the 1950s with games attracting huge crowds to Hirst Lane for visits by opponents including Amateur Cup giants Crook Town and a Hounslow Town team that included an England amateur international.

Salts won the West Riding County Cup for the first time in 1955, trouncing Lancashire Combination side Barnoldswick 7-0 in the final and kept hold of it the following season. The club were head and shoulders above their counterparts and needed an new challenge, so stepped up into the Yorkshire League, where they were able to pit their skills against professional players lining up for the reserve and A teams of Leeds United, Huddersfield Town, Sheffield United, Sheffield Wednesday, Barnsley, Rotherham United, Hull City, Halifax Town and York City, among the cream of the county's non-League sides. Success was immediate with promotion gained to Division One and the League Cup captured for good measure – beating Halifax Town Reserves 3-1 in the final. Former Tottenham and Bradford Park Avenue star Ray White took over as manager in 1956 and the older generation was replaced by a younger one, including young winger Mike Hellawell, who made such an impression that QPR made a £100 donation to spirit him away to Loftus Road, from where he went on to play for Birmingham City and Sunderland, earning two full England caps along the way.

A short period of transition followed before trophies started to roll in again, including the league cup for a second time. In the FA Amateur Cup, more good runs were enjoyed, including a 4,000 crowd to witness the demise of Stanley United, while a trip to the legendary Corinthian Casuals at Kensington Oval was memorable for two reasons. Among the home team were county cricketers Michael Willett (Surrey) and Doug Insole (Essex and England) as well as Saltaire's own Jim Laker. Perhaps overawed by that cross-sport mixture, Salts crashed 10-0.

The start of the club's demise came in the late 1950s with new manager Maurice Conroy unable to bring his Accrington Stanley experience to bear as the club finished near the bottom of the Yorkshire League and joined the West Yorkshire League for a brief spell, before returning to the West Riding County Amateur League. Success since then has been sporadic with few highlights, although when the West Riding County Amateur League was wound up in 2018, Salts had seven league titles to their name. Their final season in the competition saw them finish second in the Premier Division but their first campaign in the West Yorkshire League saw them suffer relegation to Division One. Gott said: "We want to get back in the Premier League but can't see us being able to go any higher."

The ground is in the Saltaire World Heritage Site buffer zone, meaning future development is unlikely and club committee man Simon Barraclough said: "We can't even put up a net behind the stands to stop balls going in the river, for example."

The river Aire flows behind the stands with the other touchline bordered by the Leeds-Liverpool canal but, surprisingly, the ground is rarely affected by flooding. Today's match against the appropriately named Pool was played on a soggy pitch after days of rain but excellent drainage meant a call-off was unlikely.

"That is thanks to the foresight of the original planners who built the pitch on an ash base with excellent drainage pipes down to the river," said Barraclough.

Instead of delusions of grandeur to get back the pinnacle of non-League football, Salts are now happy to be a breeding ground for future generations of players, after merging with Shipley Juniors to offer maximum chances to play the game from the very youngest age up to veteran status.

"As well as the first team in the West Yorkshire League First Division, we've also got a reserve team playing in Alliance Division One and two teams in the Craven League," said Gott. "The thirdS are mainly youngsters coming through from the junior sections, while the fourths are veterans with an age averaging about 37.

The players in all the teams are mainly local lads from Saltaire, Shipley, Baildon and Bingley. Five or six of the first team have come up through the junior system."

The link with Shipley Juniors means the club now runs dozens of teams at all ages and Gott said: "Shipley Juniors had a very successful youth system but when they reached 18 the players had nowhere to go. The u18s came to Salts and the link-up was so successful that the whole set-up moved across to become Salts Juniors. It has proved to be a merger made in heaven."

The two football pitches form part of a well-cared-for sporting complex, originally set out by Sir Titus Salt to keep the employees at his mill occupied outside of working hours. It includes a cricket field, tennis courts and bowling greens as well as a clubhouse, in normal times selling real ales (although that would have been frowned upon by tee-total Sir Titus). The football section's twin stands consist of four steps of terracing with breeze-block dug-outs on the halfway line and the changing room/tea bar complex opposite. There is no hard-standing around the post and rail surround but there are signs of very old terrace banking in the slope up to the canal.

It is still easy to imagine how a record crowd of 5,000 packed in to see a Yorkshire League match against Selby Town. A memorable picture taken from the nearby Hirst Lock gate shows thousands gathered around the football pitch for an Amateur Cup tie, with hundreds more watching the cricket on the neighbouring field. Today a crowd of about 60 was boosted by hundreds of passers-by on the canal tow path, pausing briefly to watch the action on their way to the famous Bingley five-rise locks. The Aire Valley railway line on the opposite bank carried hundreds more past the historic site.

It was hard to realise we are in the midst of a lockdown when I arrived in Saltaire with hundreds of sightseers in and around the village and Salts Mill. Queues had formed outside a variety of shops and, in normal times, a glut of bars, pubs, cafes and restaurants cater for base needs. The Salts bar clubhouse is closed at the moment but inside is a wealth of old team pictures from all the sports at the ground, plus the Barnstoneworth shirt from Palin.

Committee man Barraclough said: "I wrote to Michael Palin and his PA kindly asked him to sign a shirt for us. "He sent us one with a picture of him wearing it, together with the 'Eight-bloody-one" legend across it. I also wrote to artist David Hockney, who has local links and has a gallery in Salts Mill, but never got a reply. I'll keep trying, there's plenty of celebrities with links to the area to help publicise the club."

Chatty referee Luca Caggiano allowed me to take photos of the pictures of the team sheets on his phone before kick-off and, when I wished him a good match, joked: "I'll know I've had a good game if I don't get mentioned in any match reports."

Opinions were divided on that one after a match that saw several Pool penalty claims turned down and the visitors goalkeeper sent off.

The club produced a glossy, professional programme for first and second team games and an end-of-season review until a couple of years ago but paper souvenirs are now absent unless, like me, you can get a club official to dig out an old one from the canteen or a car boot.

Salts, in their yellow shirts and blue shorts, kicked off and made a solid start, taking a 10th-minute lead when Harry Warren, one of the products of the junior set-up, was released in the area and, as defenders stood off him, surged past them and fired a shot into the net off the post. That early goal raised my hopes of a surreal 8-bloody-1 match but, alas, it was not to be and that was the only goal of the game. Indeed, you have to go all the way back to 2011 to find the last time they did record that famous result, an 8-1 win over TVR United in a local cup tie.

Salts dominated first-half possession but failed to build on their advantage with few chances created. The white-shirted visitors relied on counter-attacks but were restricted to a few long-range efforts, easily gathered by home goalkeeper Matty Keen. Pool pushed for an equaliser after the break but always looked vulnerable on the break and chances, although still at a premium, were more forthcoming than in an often-dour first 45 minutes.

The longer the game went on, the more likely an away goal had looked but after a couple of strong penalty appeals were turned down, Pool lost their composure and concentrated more on goading the referee than worrying the opposition. Their strange continued shouts of "appeal for everything lads", probably worked against them and culminated in the last-minute dismissal of Doey, who overstepped the mark with an offensive remark to the referee, earning him a straight red card.

Gott had said before the game that Salts were playing good

football but a lack of goals could be their undoing. So it had almost proved but a 1-0 win kept manager Luke Lavery happy and maintained his team's unbeaten start to the season, going into the festive break in second place in the table.

SATURDAY AFTERNOON

May's first Saturday afternoon. From the grandstand provided by Hirst Wood Lock and along the canal bank, people watch Salts football team in their last league match of the season.
Photograph: "Shipley Times and Express."

Above - Lockdown: Fans watch from the nearby canal at Salts during the 1950s. Picture: Shipley Times & Express, courtesy of Salts FC.

Right - It's not cricket: Shipley CC's out-of-season clubhouse.

Seeing red: Pool's Andy Doey is dismissed.

16. MARLEY DREAM IS NO CHRISTMAS GHOST STORY

Monday, December 28, 2020
Marley Stadium, Keighley
Steeton 3 Nelson 0
North West Counties League, Division One North

Little did he know it but when Ben Wignall fired home a 32nd-minute opener for Steeton in their North West Counties League clash with Nelson, he was bridging a 56-year gap in the history of Keighley's Marley Stadium. Although no longer recognisable, in April 1964 the same venue witnessed a 2-2 draw for Keighley Central United against Harrogate Town Reserves to secure the Yorkshire League Division Three title.

Alas, a lack of facilities at the then-named Centre Pitch, meant promotion was refused and, instead, United dropped back into the West Yorkshire League. Within seasons they were no more; gone the same way as their forerunners Keighley Town, who had played in the Yorkshire League from 1946-48, albeit further along the Aire Valley Road at the Parkwood Stadium, later used for greyhound racing. That has been a common theme in Keighley's footballing history; going to the dogs as grand ideas of a club to rival those in neighbouring towns have been thwarted by a lack of support from the town's businesses and spectators. While Keighley rugby league club have flourished, football has never taken off at any reasonable level.

Indeed, until the arrival of Steeton from their village base six miles further up the Aire Valley, the highest ranked 'town' team was FC Sporting Keighley, plying their trade in the Premier Division of the Craven League, way down the ladder on the 14th rung of the national pyramid.

They are one of many teams to have used Marley's extensive but basic outdoor facilities over the years, numbering seven football pitches, a rugby pitch and cricket field. Teams have risen as high as the West Riding County Amateur League's Premier Division and the grand vision of local legend Trevor Hockey in 1979 raised hopes of a town team good enough to gain promotion to the Northern Premier League.

But it was not to be and, instead, the only non-League football on view for the town's 70,000 population, has been ill-fated 'loan' moves for Silsden and Steeton to the rugby club's Lawkholme Lane (Cougar Park) ground. However, that has now changed, thanks to a stroke of luck and some perfect timing.

How appropriate that in this festive week, Steeton should enjoy A Christmas Carol of a present in the form of the £280,000 redevelopment of Marley Stadium, enabling it to host non-League football for the first time in half a century. Charles Dickens' Jacob Marley was 'a good man of vision' but even he would have struggled to foresee the good fortune that befell his namesake stadium.

Steeton had moved from their cosy, but unsuitable, Summerhill Lane ground to Cougar Park to enable elevation to the North West Counties League in 2018. However, only two years into their groundshare deal, the landlords pulled the plug. The agreement had been made with a prior regime at Cougars, with the new board deciding to explore other options, leaving Steeton with the task of finding an alternative home, temporary or permanent, for 2020/21 and beyond.

Club chairman Pete Jeffrey, speaking in the Nelson programme to Emma Kennedy, took up the story: "When we were served notice to leave last year, it was a race against time to secure a suitable place for us to play the 2020/21 season. We would love to have played at Summerhill Lane but it wasn't realistic to increase the size of the pitch or build the extra facilities needed to meet the league's requirements. With the pitch so close to houses, it just wasn't feasible to build stands or install floodlights. We wanted to stay in Steeton but there wasn't anything available. We then looked at some other sites in Keighley and Utley but none of them worked for one reason or another and we were a bit short of time. When we looked at the pitch at Marley, it was clear that the site itself was ideal. Thankfully, we were on the same page as Bradford Council but it was a coincidence that when we got in touch with them, they were already looking at Marley for regeneration. It's ended up working well for us both and we've secured funding to get Marley up to speed."

Most of that funding came as part of a £15 million shake-up of Bradford's playing fields after a report into the city's sports facilities highlighted the declining state of public pitches and fields across the district. The redevelopment at Marley has seen the pitch lengthened and replaced with a new FIFA-accredited artificial surface, floodlights upgraded, with changes to the pitch barriers, fencing and access to meet Football Association requirements.

Steeton have also had to raise funds and rely on generous volunteers and sponsors to bring the ground up to the required standard, including two 50-berth stands fabricated from old freight containers, a pay booth, refreshments cabin, dug-outs and a new walkway round the pitch. The original Centre Pitch was a large ground with a grass pitch, surrounded by an athletics track, and was still in use after the demise of Central, as the major local cup final venue.

Long-standing Steeton manager Roy Mason, who took up the reins in 2006, said: "I remember playing here in a schools cup final. It was absolutely huge."

Since then the venue had been demolished, replaced by the Marley leisure centre but, coincidentally, with an artificial pitch in a similar place to where the original centre field was. That had seen better days and Mason said: "When we came to look round last year, we could see that the floodlights were there and the ground was enclosed with hard-standing, so it ticked a lot of the boxes. The biggest problem was the lack of spectator facilities and the state of the pitch as it was 15 years old and in no fit state to play football on. The council have been really helpful and we've made sure we have plenty of space around the pitch should we need to expand in the future. We've had three friendlies to sort out any glitches on and off the field and things have gone really well, it's just a shame we can't have more in for today's game," he added, with capacity limited to 150 for the competitive opener due to Covid-19 restrictions. We could easily have had double that. I don't know how deep people think my pockets are but I've had so many requests for spare tickets. Unfortunately there are none, they all went very quickly."

Mason paid tribute to the hard-working volunteers and support and generosity of local businesses. "We couldn't have made the move without them," he said. "They have been fantastic. Our volunteers and sponsors have also contributed massively."

So delighted with the facilities is Mason that he even hinted at a return to playing, albeit tongue in cheek. In an interview with James Grayson's Non-League Yorkshire website, he said: "I'm 51 but when we had the first training session here I actually got my boots back on and trained myself for a hour because the surface is fantastic. "It is without a doubt the best artificial surface I've seen. The stand is up, the changing rooms are finished, the walkways are done, the dugouts are in and we've put up advertising boards. It looks like a proper football ground."

Not that the club's previous ground at Summerhill Lane is being abandoned. "When we decided we needed to push forward, a few of the older committee were unsure but we knew if we didn't go for promotion, we'd start to stagnate," said Mason. "We're keeping the Summerhill Lane ground for our reserves and junior teams to use because we need to keep a presence in the village.

Chairman Jeffrey added: "Yes, it'll always be our original home and the pitch will still be used. We hope to introduce a women's team there in the future too. It's a three-quarter size pitch, which is perfect for developing our young players. However, the new facility is a credit to Keighley and hopefully we can attract more players to play. It's in a great location, just off the bypass, so it's accessible to everyone."

The changes at Steeton have come at lightning pace for a club that had spent its previous 112 years in local football. The formation of the club is vague but is believed to have come about for the 1910/11 season with the merger of Steeton Church Lads Brigade, Steeton Wesleyans and a previous Steeton FC, who had been playing since 1905. The new club entered two teams in the Keighley & District League, where the Church Lads had been playing since 1908, being joined the following season by the other two Steeton clubs. The new club played at The Oaks (which made way for the rebuild of an area that now includes a housing estate and the Airedale Hospital) where players often had to get washed in a nearby beck.

The first team finished second in their debut campaign in the Keighley League and won the Division Two title in 1926. Short dalliances with the South Craven Combination and Airedale & Craven Leagues before a return to the Keighley League brought immediate success. The championship title was gained in 1938 and 1939, winning it for a third time in 1955 after returning to the league following a post-war season in the Craven League.

The yo-yoing continued with the club moving back into the Craven League in 1958.The club moved to Summerhill Lane, in 1969, to the Doris Wells Memorial Field, but league success evaded them, the nearest they came being as runners-up in 1976, 1978, 1983 and 1984 before moving up the West Riding County Amateur League in 1985, winning the Division Two title in 1989 and 2001 and the Division One championship in 2010.

An early cup adventure saw them reach the final of the Keighley Charity Cup, losing 5-1 to Keighley Celtic in 1911. Two years later they went down to the same opponents 6-2 in their first Keighley FA Cup final appearance. It took a further six appearances in the district cup final before the club registered victory, beating Crosshills by a single goal in 1989. Since then, the Chevrons have lifted the cup four more times in a total of 16 appearances in the final. Their Charity Cup record looks better, however, chalking up a trophy treble in the late 30s, with two wins and a 'share' after drawing with Sutton United. After winning the West Riding County FA Trophy in 2002, the arrival of Mason as manager in 2006 coincided with a desire to push further. In 2013/14 they reached the final of the West Riding County FA County Cup but lost 5-2 in the final at Elland Road to Field.

The expansion of the North West Counties League and the earlier rise to that level of neighbours Silsden whetted the club's appetite and they were given the nod to step up, subject to getting a suitable ground. They thought they had it at Cougar Park and, after the initial shock of losing that, they are now back in a home of their own.

One person who would have been delighted to see the Marley Stadium back in use for semi-professional football is sadly no longer around. Keighley-born Trevor Hockey enjoyed a lengthy professional career in the 1960s and 70s for clubs including Bradford City, Nottingham Forest, Birmingham City, Sheffield United, Norwich City and Aston Villa, as well as gaining nine Welsh caps. He also played in the North American Soccer League against the likes of Pele.

Keighley football historian Rob Grillo, who wrote the magnificent Keighley's Soccer History book, said: "Trevor would be absolutely delighted. When he reformed the famous old Keighley Town club in 1979 he hoped to take the team into the higher echelons of non-League football. After having started life on an unenclosed pitch at Utley, the team later played on the old Marley Centre Pitch, the venue for all local cup finals and showpiece games.

"This was Keighley's Wembley Stadium, the pitch surrounded by a cinder running track that had been graced by some of the country's finest distance runners, before the whole site was torn up in the late 1980s to make way for the new Aire Valley Trunk Road, and replaced by a multi-sport all-weather pitch. Before their enforced move back to Utley, and Hockey's untimely death, Town played a few games on the adjacent Keighley RUFC pitch at Marley before that too disappeared to make way for the new road. Ironically, the same site became the site of a new football pitch, and the home ground of Keighley Phoenix some 10 years later.

"Phoenix followed Town's path and took the County Amateur title in 1990. A mainstay of that club was one Roy Mason, a man who had an entire chapter dedicated to him in my Anoraknophobia book, due to his absolute devotion to the game, and to his organisational skills. Nearly two decades on from that, Roy has himself taken Steeton into the non-League system. Ironically, Steeton have secured the much-improved and upgraded artificial surface, right where that centre pitch was."

And so to the game and, after a quick chat with manager Mason outside the changing rooms, it was into the ground via the town's Covid Test Centre, which had been set up in the car park but was not in use today. Admission was by pre-paid ticket (£5) and a quick check of my ticket and name by the ladies in the kiosk allowed entry. Straight in front was a table with the programme and some club souvenirs. The £2 programme was excellent and deserving of a place at a far higher level with lots of interesting content in a professionally produced format. Well done programme team!

To my left was one of the converted shipping containers, now holding 50 seats and not looking out of place, despite its unusual history. In the near left-hand corner sat its twin, offering shelter for 50 more fans. On the opposite side of the ground were two perspex dug outs. The pitch barriers had plenty of advertising boards and the walkways offered plenty of space to walk round, while keeping your distance in these strange times. The ground is enclosed by high fencing with opaque netting to stop external viewing, although top deck passengers on buses travelling along the Aire Valley Road could gain a free, although fleeting, glimpse of the action. After my usual circumnavigation of the pitch, it was back to the souvenir stall to spend a tenner on a Steeton scarf. It was far colder than I'd expected so it was as much to keep me warm as to show my support for the hosts – Come on you Chevrons!

Toilets are in the in adjoining leisure centre, along with a bar/ entertaining suite, with a refreshment kiosk in another converted container near the ground entrance, but closed at the moment due to coronavirus restrictions.

Steeton had hoped to make it an all-singing, all-dancing welcome to Marley for a record number of fans but the lockdown put paid to those plans as Mason told Non-League Yorkshire: "We had planned to have a pre-season game to launch it with balloons, flags, kids playing prior to us but it isn't to be. We've had to make the best of it and crack on. At least we're playing football, which is the main thing. But it is a really big occasion, not just everyone directly involved in the club but the supporters as well. They've not seen a home game of a competitive nature since February. We've gone nearly nine months without a home game. It is the end of what seems to be a very bizarre year. It is just over 12 months since we had the first meeting with the council. There's been snags in the road and we've had delays with certain things but who thought we would have the Covid scenario?"

To make up for those missed celebrations off the pitch, the Chevrons made sure it was glory all the way on the pitch with a 3-0 win over their former Football League opponents. Nelson's 10-season stint in the Football League ended 89 years ago but memories of those heady days, winning at Old Trafford and, remarkably, being the first English side to win at Real Madrid, are faithfully recorded in club legend.

Today's game is unlikely to be too fondly remembered for the Admirals though. Despite possibly just shading the balance of play and creating the majority of chances, it was the hosts' finishing power that proved decisive.

Nelson made a solid start and had the first good chance when Yves Zama tested home goalkeeper Jordan Moorhouse with a shot from the edge of the penalty area. Zama was then denied by his own team mate when a goal-bound shot was deflected away. Nelson hit a post from a free-kick and soon after Steeton made them pay with a swift and slick attack in the 32nd minute with Kayle Price crossing for Wignall to score at the far post.

Goalkeeper Jack Little's trip on Jake Townsend had the home fans screaming for a penalty but referee Lee Corns was unmoved, and possibly unsighted.

Just as it was beginning to look as if the one goal would settle it, the green-shirted hosts added a second when substitute Toby Jeffrey made up for tripping over the ball to gift it to the opposition with his first touch, by sending the ball spearing into the net from 20 yards in the 84th minute with his second touch. Nelson piled forward in search of a way back but against Steeton broke and, after a flurry of shots were fired in and blocked on the edge of the area, the ball fell nicely for man of the match Townsend to curl a superb shot into the top corner of the net from 25 yards in the 89th minute.

"I'm delighted for the lads," said manager Mason after leading his team to a second consecutive 3-0 win to continue their climb up the Division One North table. "We had to grind it out and in the first half we were not at our best. We said at half-time we needed to be better with our decision making. You only have one chance to make a first impression and there was a lot of people watching Steeton for the first time today. It was important they left here with a good feeling and I think people will have really enjoyed that."

You're right Roy – we did!

Opening day: Match programme and ticket for Steeton's competitive debut at Marley.

Touchline patrol: Steeton manager Roy Mason.

Who are ya? Early arrivals at the Marley Stadium.

Signs of the times

Above - Kiveton - No entry: One way of keeping a clean sheet I suppose!

Right - Foul language: Straight to the point at Kellingley.

Below - Spoilt for choice: Pub adverts at Brighouse.

Eternal support: Tributes at Doncaster Rovers.

Sup up lads: Drinking in the atmosphere at Ripon.

17. MAIN ROAD TO GLORY

Friday, April 2, 2021
Miners Welfare Ground, Edlington Lane, New Edlington
Yorkshire Main 1 Askern Miners 2
Doncaster Saturday League, Premier Division

At last! Five days short of a century of days since my trip to Keighley I was able to resume my journey following a slight easing of the latest lockdown. Fans were still banned from attending but the luxury of a press pass gave me the opportunity to get pitchside again.

There's a strong case to be made for coal being key to football in much of Yorkshire. The discovery of rich deposits of the black gold heralded a huge influx of miners from across the country and many of them brought their favourite sport with them, to what had been a rugby stronghold.

While the M62 corridor remains mainly rugby league territory, the A1 boasts a solid round-ball pedigree on its run through South Yorkshire, thanks to those pioneers.

The opening of coal mines in and around the Doncaster area brought an rush of experienced colliers from further south. That was definitely the case in Edlington, or 'Edlo' as it is known to the locals, where a whole new village was built to house the men and their families, many who came from Derbyshire and the Potteries. Work on sinking the shafts at Edlington Colliery began in 1909, with its name changed after two years to Yorkshire Main. By 1923 it employed more than 3,000 men. Closed in 1985, just a year after recording a profit of £4.5million, all signs of the pit have long gone.

All that remains is a proud heritage, the Welly (miners welfare club) and the former colliery welfare sports grounds, now in the care of CISWO (Coal Industry Social Welfare Organisation – the coal mining charity), with the former winding wheel at its entrance ensuring passing traffic are given a reminder of what once was. The pit itself is undergoing a transformation into Warmsworth

Gate, the site for 375 homes, a pub, landscaping and public open spaces, next to Edlington Pit Wood Country Park.

In the mine's hey day, such was its success, it was graced in 1953 by the presence of royalty with HRH Prince Phillip. The Duke of Edinburgh spent time underground to see the conditions the men were working under and paid tribute to their efforts.

Time above ground was valuable for the miners and the men soon set up their own sports teams with benevolent owners providing facilities for bowls, cricket, rugby and, of course football. Edlington Welfare FC became Edlington Rangers and players from the village made an immediate impression and were soon on their way to greater things.

Even though Yorkshire Main and their predecessors have never hit the big time, rarely playing above local league level, the village has a rich footballing heritage. Leading the way was World Cup winner Ron Flowers. Born in the village in 1934, the former Edlington Top School and Grammar School pupil spent his junior days with Wolverhampton Wanderers' nursery side Wath Wanderers and played as an amateur with Doncaster Rovers before joining the great Wolves side of the 1950s/60s, earning three Football League titles (plus two runners-up honours), and the FA Cup, scoring 37 goals in 515 appearances in midfield.

He was later player-manager at Northampton Town and Telford United. After making his England u23 debut as a 19-year-old, Flowers gained full international honours at 20, picking up 49 caps and scoring 10 times between 1955 and 1966. He made a record 40 consecutive appearances between 1958 and 1963 and was the scorer of England's first European Championships goal, against France at Hillsborough in 1962. He was in Alf Ramsay's squad for the 1966 World Cup finals and put on stand-by to play when Jack Charlton fell ill on the eve of the tournament but the Leeds man recovered and Flowers was unused.

Awarded the MBE earlier this year for services to football, Flowers is now 87 and a Wolves vice-president, as well as president of the club's former players' association.

However, Ron was not the first Flowers to blossom in Edlington. He was following in the bootprints of his uncle George Flowers.

Although born in Staffordshire in 1907, the elder Flowers moved to Edlington as a child and played for the Colliery Welfare team until 1927. The half-back then made the short trip to Doncaster Rovers, chalking up 149 appearances and helping the team to the Division Three North title in 1935. He later played for Bradford Park Avenue, Tranmere Rovers and Rochdale. A league title was also earned for Doncaster Rovers by Ron's younger brother John, who was also born in Edlington. After three years with Stoke City, Flowers junior spent five seasons at Belle Vue, recording 164 appearances, including a memorable 1968/9 campaign that culminated in winning the Division Four title. He later played for Port Vale and was married to world darts champion Maureen Flowers.

The Flowers footballing dynasty continues to this day in the shape of Ron's grandson Harry. Although not directly linked to Edlington, he was born in Stafford, he is a Doncaster Rovers fan, thanks to his granddad's roots. After starting his career with Burnley, the young centre back has since played at senior non-League level with Guiseley, Solihull, Kidderminster, Brackley and Curzon Ashton, as well as Larne in Northern Ireland.

Another Edlington Rangers old boy gained legendary status with Newcastle United. Joe Harvey started his career as an inside forward with the team, while working as an apprentice machinist at the pit, before moving to Wolves. He then played for Bournemouth, Bradford City, Aberdeen and Dundee United before eventually joining Newcastle in 1945, making his name as a tough-tackling half back. He remained at St James' Park on-and-off for the majority of half a century, becoming the last manager to lead the Geordies to a major trophy – winning the Inter-Cities Fairs Cup in 1969.

As a player, he turned out in the black and white stripes from 1945-53, scoring 12 times in 224 games and captaining them to the FA Cup in 1951 and 52. He left Tyneside to coach Crook Town to the 1955 FA Amateur Cup and then learned the managerial ropes with Barrow and Workington before returning to the Magpies. He was in the hot seat from 1962-75 and because the club's most successful manager, winning the Division Two title in 1965, the Fairs Cup and Anglo-Italian Cup and leading them to the 1974

FA Cup final, where they were beaten 3-0 by a Liverpool side for who another Doncaster lad and eventual Newcastle hero, Kevin Keegan, scored twice.

Harvey was rarely seen without a cigarette in his hand and, as a player, legend has it he would warm-up with a couple of pints of Guinness. Industrial language remained with him throughout his career and his long-term captain Bobby Moncur recalled that Fairs Cup win over Ujpest Dozsa in Budapest. United were struggling to hold on to the lead they had built in the first leg and, at half-time, according to Moncur, Harvey strolled into the dressing room, fag in hand and said (with expletives omitted): "What's the matter? They're foreigners. Just score a goal and they'll collapse like a pack of cards." Which is what happened.

Harvey, a former PT instructor and Company Sergeant Major in the Royal Artillery, had his own method of dealing with tricky opponents, telling United defenders: "See how fast that centre-forward can limp."

After stepping down as manager, Harvey stayed with the club, working on the backroom staff and as chief scout. He died in 1989.

Edlington Rangers players B Chappell and P Todd also moved into the Football League, with Portsmouth, but failed to make a career of it, as did former Edlington Victoria Road schoolboy Sinclair, who went to Barnsley, while coming the other way, Stan Brookes, finished his career with Yorkshire Main after starring in almost 300 games for Doncaster Rovers and Belgian side KV Mechelen in the 1970s and 80s.

Playing separately at the welfare ground throughout the decades have been Edlington White Stars and two of their old boys made a name for themselves in the professional ranks. Glynn and Ian Snodin were both juniors at the club before enjoying lengthy success at many clubs, including Doncaster Rovers, Sheffield Wednesday, Leeds United, Everton, Sunderland, Oldham Athletic, Rotherham United, Barnsley, Scarborough and Hearts. Both went into the management ranks, adding their knowledge to the coaching set-ups at Carlisle, Doncaster, Southampton, West Ham, Huddersfield and Charlton Athletic, as well as the Northern Ireland and England u21 international sides.

A Leeds United legend was also a regular visitor to the Welfare ground in the 1990s. Billy Bremner spent many Sunday mornings watching local youngsters, while he was manager at Doncaster. Bremner lived in nearby Clifton and his funeral was held in Old Edlington in 1997.

Edlington is also the final resting place of a long unsung hero. Arthur Wharton was the world's first black professional player but was buried in a pauper's grave after dying at Springwell Sanatorium in Balby in 1930. He was born in the Gold Coast (now Ghana) in 1865 but moved to England in 1882. He was an all-round sportsman and played rugby union and cricket to a high standard as well as equalling the amateur 100-yard sprint world record and being a highly-rated cyclist.

But it was as a footballer he made his name where, despite that lightning speed, he played in goal for Darlington, Preston North End, Rotherham Town, Sheffield United and Stockport County, among others. He was the original 'crazy' goalkeeper, pulling off some incredible tricks. One fan recalled: "In a match between Rotherham and Sheffield Wednesday I saw Wharton jump, take hold of the crossbar, catch the ball between his legs, and cause three onrushing forwards to fall into the net."

He regularly played as a makeshift defender, knowing his speed would enable him to get back between the posts if the need arose. Wharton also became known for crouching next to one of the posts and waiting for a shot to be taken before diving into position. He retired from football in 1902 and worked at various collieries before becoming a haulage worker at Yorkshire Main pit. A campaign by the Football Unites, Racism Divides group saw Wharton's grave given a headstone in 1997 and in 2003 he was honoured in the English Football Hall of Fame in recognition of the impact he made on the game.

While players from the village have hit the heights, that has not been the case for the local football team. Edlington Rangers played just one season in the FA Amateur Cup (beating Hathersage 2-1 in the 1928/9 qualifying round before losing 5-1 at Pilkington Recs). It was another 62 years before the club appeared at national level again, and once again it was for a single season, with Yorkshire

Main losing 2-1 at home to Sheffield FC in the first round of the 1990/91 FA Vase, having beaten Kimberley Town (2-0) and Hatfield Main (2-0) in the preliminary rounds.

Nowadays, Main are plying their trade in the Doncaster Saturday League, just pleased to still be active after several fraught years. It used to be a case of walking round the carefully nurtured cricket ground to reach Main's ground from the car park in front of the Welfare Club. The immaculate wicket was out of bounds and to step on to the hallowed turf would brings yells of outrage from the ever-watchful groundsman. Not so now, the grass is used for junior football with Edlington White Stars u9s taking on their Rotherham Schools counterparts on my visit. The cricket pavilion is boarded up and the circular path around the ground overgrown and dotted with old car tyres.

The football ground is behind high, spiked, fences and the changing rooms and tea bar building is in a separate compound, with another layer of security fencing to keep out unwanted visitors. There is much to protect with the ground looking spick and span after a lot of time and effort has been put into sprucing it up. A combined standing terrace and two dug-outs are on the near side, with access to the pitch through the back of the smartly painted gleaming white structure, resplendent with sponsors' name and club logo. A covered terrace opposite has standing either side, and again the liberal use of white paint is obvious. Apart from those small patches of terracing, the only other non-grass area is behind the far goal, where a small stand used to sit but the area is now out of bounds to fans, along with half the changing room side. Three crush barriers on the railway side await the arrival of fans when lockdown restrictions lift, with one more half-hidden in the grass.

A small group of spectators had managed to find a vantage point from the corner of the cricket ground, looking over the fence into the ground – keen to witness some live action after the two-month shutdown of all footballing activity. Chairman Matthew Wynne, a former player and manager, was busy filling holes in the pitch when I arrived, after receiving a hearty greeting from the two men on the entrance gate and completing the usual paperwork and sanitation.

Wynne was pleased to be back in action and admitted lockdown had been tough for the club. However, they had made good use of the unexpected mid-season break. "The lockdown has been hard; not having football to look forward to, but it has meant we've been busy giving the ground a facelift and it looks well for it," said Wynne, who wears multiple hats – he is also the club secretary, treasurer, fixture secretary, membership secretary, press officer, webmaster and, once the match started, was regularly scurrying over the fence to recover misdirected balls as a makeshift ball boy.

"You do wonder if it is all worth it when fans can't come in," he said. "We're missing the bit of atmosphere that even a few people can bring but, hopefully, we'll be able to let them back in a couple of weeks. Until then, I chat over the fence to those who do come to see what they can from the corner of the old cricket ground. They're all regulars and I've known them for years. I came here as a player in 1994/5 but got a bad injury. I've stuck about ever since, first as manager and now as chairman, plus the rest! We're hopeful our crowds will go up when fans are eventually allowed to return. Before Covid we'd get about 30 watching us but that doubled between lockdowns and I'm sure we'd have had between 100 and 200 tonight if we'd been allowed to open the gates."

Wynne and his small band of committee men – now numbering four after struggling along with just two – have done a remarkable job. "It was just me and two committee men – Ged Kelly and George Hanlon – but we've got another member now, Chewy Baccus, who runs Firefly, whose adverts are all round the ground. The manager Paul Roidl is also on the committee and my daughter helps out in the tea bar – when we can open it."

"Firefly is a local charity that provides transportation for cancer patients to hospitals for treatment. We have recently formed a connection and to support them, we have provided opportunities for them to promote their brand on our stands and fencing. We hope that this is going to develop further, whereby we can host fundraising events and competitions for them."

Yorkshire Main have run just one team for many years but have now opened up opportunities at opposite ends of the age spectrum. "We're starting an over-35s side and a new u20s," said Wynne.

"We've never had a junior section. White Stars have always been a separate entity but we are hoping to build bridges with them through the new team. We also play host to Doncaster ISG, the Polish International School team, in our league. They've been here three years and are a good bunch of lads."

My main memory of previous visits to the ground was the huge chains that formed the pitch barrier. Thick as your arm and rusted solid, they were stronger than any steel rails and you only leaned on them once, they were filthy! Although the solid concrete bases they were hanging from remain, the actual chains have gone. "They were winding gear from the old pit but we had to get rid of them because people kept pinching bits," said Wynne. "Dennis Tymon had run the club for many years and was a real servant to the club," said Wynne, paying tribute to the former secretary. "When he decided to leave – he was in this 80s by then – it was a struggle to carry on.

"He thought we'd played our last game when he came to tell us we couldn't afford to pay the match officials. We'd also had a break in and the shower roof was damaged. Damp got in and the showers, dressing rooms and tea bar roof were all caving in. It all looked grim."

In my Soap Stars and Burst Bubbles book, Tymon lamented the bad timing of the pit closure and how it had affected the club. "When the colliery closed in 1985 the club was put under severe strain," he said.

A lack of finance and new demands on ground facilities saw the club drop back to junior level but Tymon added: "If the pit had stayed open another 12 months, we'd have kept our place in the Northern Counties East League because we would have had the floodlights and better facilities. But Yorkshire Main was the first pit to shut and that left us high and dry in more ways than one – I was an electrical engineer there and lost my job."

However, the club and its small band of volunteers have managed to stay afloat and Wynne said: "Somehow we've managed to keep going and things are looking much better. Luckily we got money from the Football Foundation and did lots of fund-raising so managed to repair that damage.

"We'd love to get back to the Northern Counties East League and now have a lot in place that we didn't when we had to leave the league before. It has been hard work with just the three of us. It was taking four or five weeks just to cut the hedges!"

The club's tea bar is a shrine to the footballing history of the village and club. As well as Yorkshire Main and their predecessors Edlington Rangers and Edlington Welfare, there are also images of Victoria Road School team, Top School, Edlington White Stars, Edlington Celtic and a 1926 ladies group shot. Cuttings about Ron Flowers and Joe Harvey also tell the story of the village's most famous sons.

On the pitch today, a last-gasp 'slow motion' strike from Sam Corner gave visitors Askern all the points as football returned from lockdown. While some leagues had been declared null and void and others were running cup competitions to fill the gap to the end of the season, the Doncaster Saturday League was carrying on with its scheduled fixture list.

With dressing rooms closed due to coronavirus restrictions, players and match officials arrived ready-changed and pre-match team talks were delivered on the pitch. That from the Askern manager must have been inspirational because it took them all of 58 seconds to open the scoring. Chris Hancock was left unmarked on the edge of the penalty area from a long throw and when the ball was headed on, he sent it rocketing past goalkeeper Jamie Qualter with a stunning left-foot volley.

The black-and-white shirted visitors almost doubled their lead after 11 minutes but this time Qualter was equal to the task, saving well with his legs. The floodlights flickered into action a minute later but, with a third of the bulbs not working, it left a chequer-board-effect on the pitch. Main came close to equalising after 19 minutes when Callum Wootton broke clear on the right. His shot from the corner of the penalty area beat goalkeeper Richard Groom but bounced off the foot of the far post with no other forward on hand to convert.

On the stroke of half-time, an Askern shot was blocked in the goal area with the visitors appealing for handball to no avail.

The second half lacked the spark of the first with referee Blaike

Watkins needing to be on his toes to break up several 'comings-together' as emotions ran high. It was all square after 72 minutes when Main broke away after withstanding a lengthy spell of pressure and the ball was swept to the back post for Nathan Ashbridge to side foot home.

The points looked as if they were going to be shared when Askern missed a good opportunity for the winner after 86 minutes when a corner was cleared off the line and the follow-up effort slammed against the bar. However, in the 89th minute, a long ball caught out the Main defence and Corner won the race to the edge of the penalty area to flick the ball past Qualter with an outstretched toe. The ball seemed to bounce towards goal in slow motion and the first Corner, who fell with his back to goal, knew he had scored was when he was mobbed by his delighted team mates.

Despite three minutes of stoppage time, there was no way back for the hosts and the 'Mines Derby' honours went to Askern.

Digging in: Coal mining provides a central thread for much of this book.

Flashback: Cuttings in the Yorkshire Main clubhouse.

Locked out: Fans were banned again.

18. OH LITTLETOWN OF LEGENDS

Wednesday, April 7, 2021
Beck Lane, Heckmondwike
Littletown 4 Route One Rovers 2
Yorkshire Amateur League, Supreme Division

How Huddersfield Town could have done with the input of their Beck Lane legends at Norwich City the night before I visited the home of Littletown. The Terriers were put to the sword, crashing 7-0 at Carrow Road, and would have paid millions for the input of their much-lauded predecessors.

Beck Lane now hosts Yorkshire Amateur League action but back in the 1950s was the home of the current Championship club's junior teams. One memorable FA Youth Cup tie in the 1956/7 season attracted a crowd of between 2,000 and 5,000, depending on which source you believe, to watch a teenage Denis Law take on his future team-mates from Manchester United. A watching Matt Busy was so impressed he is reputed to have made a £10,000 offer for the Scottish youngster on the spot.

That was turned down and Busby eventually had to fork out a British record transfer fee of £115,000 to Torino five years later for the Lawman, after Huddersfield had received £55,000 from Manchester City, before his move to Italy. The money Town received for Law was spent on the club's first floodlights at their Leeds Road home, erected in 1961. Bizarrely those lights came seven years after Beck Lane had already had its own illumination added.

Also catching the eye in those long-gone days were the likes of Ray Wilson, Les Massie and Bill McGarry, all under the watchful eye of Bill Shankly, who, as assistant manager to his old friend and former Preston North End teammate Andy Beattie, was keen to nurture their talents, ahead of stepping into the Town hotseat himself in November 1956, where he continued to keep an eye on the Terriers' teenage talent.

The former Carlisle, Grimsby and Workington boss had been brought in by Beattie to look after Town's Reserve team in the Central League and juniors, in the Northern Intermediate League, who played at Beck Lane. Shankly eventually left West Yorkshire to make his name over the Pennines, creating the Anfield legacy at Liverpool.

Town's move to Beck Lane came after an 'A' team had been formed in 1929 to play in the Yorkshire League. The fixture schedule at Leeds Road was full and home games were played at Methley and Savile Town before they started to rent Beck Lane in 1934, buying it 17 years later.

A player who remembered those days well was 1966 World Cup-winning left back Ray Wilson. In an interview with the Huddersfield Examiner in 2013, he recalled: "In my early years, I spent as much time at Beck Lane as I did at Leeds Road. I played there for both the juniors and the A team, and the Yorkshire League especially was a great environment in which to learn the game There were some really good sides and many of the teams were from the big coal mines. I remember blokes coming out on to the pitch with their faces still black with dust. They were tough lads and you needed to keep your wits about you!"

Wilson won 30 England caps before moving to Everton in 1964 and recalled travelling to work at Beck Lane on the bus. "Young players were signed as members of the groundstaff, and we used to get all kinds of jobs to do. One was to go to Beck Lane and help take care of the pitch, and it meant taking the bus there and back."

After starting in the Yorkshire League, Wilson's near 500-game professional career also ended in that league, turning out for Selby Town in the 1970s, where he reputedly threw his boots across the dressing room after a pasting by a visiting right-winger, stating "That's it, I've finished." He went on to enjoy a long post-football career as a funeral director.

Another player who told the Huddersfield Examiner's Doug Thomson about his Beck Lane memories was Les Massie. Like Law, the Scottish striker came to the West Riding from Aberdeen, joining two years earlier, in 1953 as an 18 year old.

"I played for both the juniors and third team at Beck Lane, and

I can still picture the place very clearly," he said. "Myself and a number of the other players used to spend much of the close-season working at the ground. In those days, our wages used to fall out of season, so we'd top them up by sorting out the pitch and sprucing the place up by painting and lopping trees and bushes. John Coddington, Bob Ledger, Brian Gibson and Oliver Conmy were other members of the work gang and we were under the supervision of Jack Anderson, who was Town's trainer at that time. I can remember the five of us walking up and down the pitch, raking then re-seeding, and a few times I ended up in the beck after which the ground was named, fishing out footballs and goodness knows what else!"

Frank Worthington and Trevor Cherry were among the later generation of Town players who honed their skills for international duty at Beck Lane, before the club left in the early 1990s.

Heckmondwike also has links with other football super stars, including Stanley Matthews. The Heckmondwike Co-operative Boot and Shoe Works was housed in Brunswick Mill in the town. Its 400 workers made safety footwear as well as football boots, including the specially designed, ultra lightweight 'Goliaths' worn by the Stoke and England flying winger.

Although Shankly, Law, Wilson, Massie, Worthington, Cherry and Matthews, will be recognised by fans of certain vintages, the ground's first big name star is largely forgotten. John Sutcliffe was remarkable in that the goalkeeper played for England having previously earned international honours playing rugby. His one rugby appearance was against the touring New Zealand Natives in 1889, with the Heckmondwike player scoring a try and a conversion for five points in a 7-0 win. When his club were suspended by the RFU over allegations of professionalism, he switched codes to football and gained his first international cap while with Bolton Wanderers, becoming the last player to represent England rugby union and football teams. Sutcliffe went on to gain four more caps between 1893 and 1903, winning Home International honours four times. He represented the Football League five times and also played for Millwall, Manchester United, Plymouth Argyle and Southend United. He eventually moved back to his native Yorkshire, turning out for South Kirkby before returning to

Heckmondwike in 1913, this time to play the round ball game. He later managed Dutch side Vitesse Arnhem and worked as a coach for Bradford City.

In its hey day, as well as floodlights, Beck Lane boasted a stand at the railway end, changing rooms and turnstiles. Hidden behind a big fence and gate on a narrow bend next to the railway tunnel in Cornmill Lane, all the current ground can boast is a covered terrace along the former allotments side and a couple of portable buildings serving as a tea bar and changing room block. But all that will change, if Littletown's committee have their way.

Colin Bould has been with the club for 49 years, since starting as a 20 year-old player. However, he is not the longest serving member, that honour belongs to Derek Senior, who lives up to his surname with almost 57 years at the club, joining three years after they were formed. Bould, a retired plasterer, said: "The club started in 1960/1 so is celebrating its 60th anniversary this season. We were just a little kick-about team but were always a good side. Our first pitch was at Stanley Park and then we played behind the baths, towards Cleckheaton, before coming to Beck Lane about 21 years ago.

"We started in the Spen Valley League and were in the West Riding County Amateur League for many seasons before joining the Yorkshire Amateur League. Huddersfield Town were happy for us to play at Beck Lane and look after it in lieu of rent."

When Town put the ground up for sale about eight years ago, Littletown swiftly made an offer with Bould and several other club members chipping in with the necessary funding. "We've put up fences and done lots of tidying up," he said. "We're in the process of putting up netting to stop balls going into the beck but the next major development will be new changing rooms. After that, we hope to put up floodlights. We just want to make the ground as good a standard as we can. I suppose it could be good enough for the Northern Counties East League eventually but the lack of parking will always hold us back. It used to have huge soil banks all round and quite a crowd could be catered for but now, on a good day, we can get 100-or-more down."

There is plenty of space round the ground for future development, although the club is hampered by Spen Beck, alongside the far touchline, and the old railway embankment, now a cycle path, behind the near goal. New housing sits behind the stand side. Like Massie and countless other players and officials in decades past, the ground lives up to its name with a constant reminder of where it came from throughout tonight's game. Bould was later seen brandishing a large pole with a net on the end of it in a vain attempt to reach several balls sitting in the beck, which is a 10-foot drop just a few yards from the touchline. A willing volunteer, ladder and wellington boots were needed to complete the task.

Similar to the Doncaster Saturday League, for my previous match, the Yorkshire Amateur League has decided to continue their season and have extended the fixture list to the end of June. It means Littletown have an extra couple of months to squeeze in their remaining 20 games but that will involve many midweek encounters. Tonight's match kicked-off at 6.30pm and only the decision by referee Jack Andrews to reduce each half by five minutes ensured it finished in something resembling daylight.

Littletown manager Jonathan Ginnelly will have been happy to see his side romp into a 3-0 lead inside half-an-hour as visitors Route One Rovers rather misunderstood their name, deciding to play lots of 'tippy-tappy' football in their own penalty area and were caught out numerous times. Only goalkeeper Imran Yousaf and some wasteful finishing saved them from a real walloping. After only eight minutes Yousaf pounced low to his right to keep out a close-range effort but the rebound fell awkwardly for him and Scott Lightowler hammered in the loose ball from a matter of feet for the opener.

The claret and light blue-kitted hosts swarmed forward and only some desperate defending kept them at bay until the 26th minute when a long through ball released centre forward Thomas Ramsden and he tucked the ball past the goalkeeper from the edge of the area. The first chance for the visitors came a minute later when Danny Hussain burst through on goal but home goalkeeper Luke Fozard blocked the ball with his legs on the edge of the box. It was a case of normal business resumed after 31 minutes when Williams fired over a free-kick and Bolton powered though the mass of bodies in the box to crash in a header for the third goal.

A lapse in the home defence gave Route One an unexpected way back when a scramble saw Fozard keep out two efforts before the ball broke loose for Sinmi Oyebanji to tap in.

The three-goal home advantage was restored five minutes after the break when Williams again set up Bolton, this time with a corner kick that the powerful centre back despatched with the same ease as the earlier free-kick. The all-grey kit of the visitors was fast disappearing as the gloom descended and they started to enjoy more of the game as the hosts struggled to pick up their moves. They pulled a goal back after 51 minutes when Hussain made a good run and pulled the ball back for Zak Khan to score but, despite creating several more chances, they were unable to narrow the gap further and, with the sun having set and car lights illuminating the changing room area, referee Andrews called a halt.

That was unlike the remarkable 2001 game against Storthes Hall at the ground that was eventually abandoned due to bad light. The cup tie had finished all square and the 'deciding' penalty shoot-out was tied at 17-17 when the match official eventually gave up.

Littletown are the latest in a long list of teams to have played at Beck Lane. Originally a rugby ground, its first tenants were Heckmondwike rugby club, who were formed in the 1870s. They joined the Northern Union (later rugby league) in 1896 and attracted a crowd of almost 4,000 for the derby with Liversedge at Beck Lane, where they had been playing for at least 10 years.

That club folded in 1902 but members were determined to keep sport at Beck Lane and quickly formed a team to play the association code. Heckmondwike Casuals soon dropped their suffix but their FA Amateur Cup debut proved a non-starter, scratching from their tie at York St Clements in 1904 and they never competed in it again. They had a longer association with the FA Cup and, according to Tony Brown's excellent FA Cup Complete Results book, played in 23 ties from 1905 until 1915. Their debut brought a 1-0 defeat at home to Mirfield United but they gained revenge two seasons later, winning 3-1 against their neighbours, going on to beat Darfield United and Castleford Town before going down 5-3 at home to Denaby United in the third qualifying round. They repeated that feat in 1908/09 before scratching when drawn away to Football League side Bradford Park Avenue.

Ironically, one of their earliest FA Cup visitors to Beck Lane were Huddersfield Town. September 1909, marked the Terriers first-ever FA Cup appearance and they made an immediate impression, romping to an 11-0 preliminary-round win.

Heckmondwike's final season in the Cup proved to be their most successful. They beat Castleford Town in a replay and saw off Rothwell White Rose before gaining another replay win over South Kirkby Colliery. That set up a fourth qualifying round home tie against Shirebrook but the Derbyshire side proved too strong, going through 2-0.

Heckmondwike were prominent in the West Yorkshire Cup, a predecessor of the West Riding County FA Senior Cup. They reached the final of the 1904 and 1906 competitions, losing to Altofts and Bradford City respectively, and both the 1905 and 1907 semi-finals, going out to Mirfield and Leeds City. Spurred on by those cup exploits, Heckmondwike became founder members of the Yorkshire Combination in 1910. Opponents included Goole Town, Scarborough and York City, plus the reserve teams of the two Bradford clubs, as well as neighbours Mirfield United and Morley.

That league folded after five seasons but the club took a major step to join the first teams of Rotherham County and Town (later United), Chesterfield, Halifax Town, Scunthorpe United, Doncaster Rovers and York City as well as several other professional clubs' reserve teams in the Midland League. Unfortunately, the Wikes lasted only one campaign, being expelled at the 1915 AGM for failing to play games on the agreed dates. Even though the hardships of World War One were causing problems, Heckmondwike gained few friends with a string of misdemeanours, as reported by David Webster in his Historical Look at the Midland Counties League 1889-1982 book. These included turning up with just one player to take on Lincoln City, making up their XI from members of the crowd who they 'signed' before kick-off. They did the same thing at Worksop, when they arrived with only three players, despite having received 12 passes for free rail travel to the ground. Heckmondwike frequently failed to pay match officials and ignored fines issued by the league and were ejected, never to be seen again.

Since then, various teams have made Beck Lane their home, including Norristhorpe Nipps, Heckmondwike Spen, Spenborough and Rendons, while the ground was also used regularly for cup semi-finals and finals.

Big deal: Goliath boots, as worn by Stanley Matthews, were made in Heckmondwike.

Just for laughs: Hilarity in the Littletown dugout.

Dipping in: Colin Bould prepares to net some stray balls.

19. THEY'VE GOT GOD ON THEIR SIDE

Saturday, April 24, 2021, 10.30am
Fearnville Fields, Oakwood Lane, Leeds
Life United 0 Bridge Community Church 1
Yorkshire Christian League, Division One

They celebrated the winning goal as if they'd won the World Cup and, for many of the Bridge Community Church players, that was an appropriate analogy. Many of the team are asylum seekers, discovering a better life after escaping murderous and inhumane conditions in their home countries, now discovering that God is indeed on their side.

Opponents Life United base their team ethos on raising awareness of mental health among men and these are just some of the many humanitarian attributes on display in the Yorkshire Christian League.

Formed in 1993, the league was originally for church teams but has gradually expanded to offer help and support across the communities in which they are based. Life manager and league committee member Ben Hilton said: "The original aim was to get more people going to church through the football community. You don't have to be a Christian to play in the league, we are here for all the community."

However, any thoughts matches in the league would be all "after you vicar" with cucumber sandwiches and tea in bone china cups for the half-time break were dispelled in the opening minutes of today's game with a series of crunching tackles. The players swear, curse and niggle the referee just as much as in any other football game and the league's expansion shows that more and more teams are buying into that character.

Down to 12 teams in two divisions this season due to Covid-19, next season will kick-off in September with 20 teams already signed up across Yorkshire.

Hilton said: "The perception some people have of what a

Christian Football League is about is all wrong. As I said anyone can play, it's all about community involvement. Some of our lads play Sunday football, others are in 'regular' teams on a Saturday afternoon, while one of our goalkeepers, Charlie Isherwood, claims to be an all-rounder and is wicketkeeper for a cricket team, often going straight off to play behind the wickets after a game with us in the morning.

We've got some players who have played at a decent standard – Joel Dixon was with Blyth Spartans in their 2015 FA Cup run, which took them to a third round meeting with Birmingham City. A few others have played quite high up but drifted away from the game until they got the chance to come back into it with us. We've got about 40 players signed up but can get 50 or 60 down for training."

Bridge are playing all their games at home this season due to a lack of transport. Fearnville Leisure Centre is closed but the car park is in use as a Covid-19 test centre so the football car park is now the entrance road and was already full of Life players, changing next to their cars, when I arrived. In contrast, the Bridge players arrived in dribs and drabs all carrying obligatory rucksacks and jogging to make kick-off with excited grins on their faces and animated conversations taking place.

The camaraderie among the Bridge players was immediately apparent, even though, due to the nature of their background, they tend to field virtually a different team every week.

The ground is one of several sports pitches on the Fearnville playing fields, overlooking a series of tower blocks with the skyscrapers of Leeds on the horizon.

The Bridge Community Church is actually in Burmantofts, an inner-city area, but all their players live within walking (or jogging!) distance of the ground.

A club statement reads: "We are unlike any other team in the league, fielding 50 per cent asylum seekers, allowing them get into sports, in turn helping them create friends and build a sense of pride in representing something."

Burmantofts is noticeable for its 1960s high-rise flats, but the church's history dates back more than 100 years to the former

Mount Tabor Pentecostal Church, which attracted congregations of up to 2,000.

However, the football team is more of an outreach service and player-secretary Joe Pickering said: "The majority of our players are from around the Gipton, Fearnville and Burmantofts area. They're all asylum seekers basically, aside from about four or five of them. The area has a lot of asylum seekers from African countries, with limited or no English, so the team offers the chance for many of them to get involved in football. It gives them something to do otherwise it's so easy to get in with the wrong crowd.

"They face a lot of the general issues asylum seekers face. We have a large core of Eritreans who came to the UK to escape persecution for being Christian. We are helping them through sports to bring them into the community more, helping them create social groups and build relationships with a number of people."

The transient nature of the Bridge team was quickly evident as they withstood an early bombardment from their blue and black stripe-shirted opponents. In the first minute Nath Evans broke clear and only a brave block by Bridge goalkeeper Fabio Intumbo kept him out. Within seconds, Intumbo again had to be quick off the blocks to deny another effort after a poor back pass exposed him.

A delightful finish from Evans looked to have broken the deadlock after 20 minutes when he chipped the ball over Intumbo but his celebrations were cut short by the referee's whistle for offside. The hard-working Intumbo then pulled off the save of the match, throwing himself high to his left to claw a vicious 20-yard shot from the Life no.18 round a post.

Life had a second goal disallowed after 51 minutes when Billy Williams headed in a free-kick but was penalised for a push. Meron Araya, one of two Bridge players bearing a no.3 shirt tried his luck from long range after 56 minutes but his shot flew narrowly over the bar. The man-bunned Joey Davey squandered a great chance for Life after 71 minutes when he got on the end of a corner but somehow managed to head the ball over the bar from on the goalline.

As the game wore on, Life started to tire and Bridge grew more cohesive. Only a desperate save from Bigamore preserved his clean sheet in the 82nd minute when he parried a shot and then managed to toe-poke the ball away from danger between the legs of a striker who was poised to tap the ball home. There was no let-off for the bespectacled custodian after 84 minutes though. A high through ball saw him lose out in a challenge with a muscular forward and the ball popped free for the waiting Semir Gebremedihn to knock the ball into the vacant net, sparking incredible celebrations scenes, with him somehow managing to lose his shirt. A repeat five minutes later again saw Bigamore spill the ball under pressure and the same opponent once more found the net, but this time he was denied by the referee for a foul on the goalkeeper.

Three minutes of stoppage time failed to be enough for Life to save a point but, despite an often fiery encounter in which the referee regularly had to step in to quell rising tempers, the players left the pitch amid friendly banter, with the man in black playing his part, both giving and receiving.

Fearnville is a new ground for Bridge, as Pickering explained: "We played at Gledhow last season thanks to my dad's team helping us out by letting us use their pitch when they played away. We moved to Fearnville this season because our manager worked for the council and was able to get us the pitch."

That ground at Gledhow holds a resonance with both of today's teams. Leeds United legend Albert Johanneson lived in Gledhow Towers. He was Don Revie's first signing, in April 1961, before going on to become the first black player to play in an FA Cup final in 1965 when Leeds lost 2-1 to Liverpool at Wembley. He made 172 appearances for the Whites, scoring 48 goals, before moving on to a spell with York City where he scored three goals in 26 appearances.

Life after football did not treat the South African well, and he became somewhat of a recluse, suffering from a severe addiction to alcohol. Johanneson died alone of meningitis and heart failure in 1995. His body lay undiscovered for a week in his flat.

While Bridge are concentrating on helping refugees find their feet in a strange country, their opponents focus attention on men's mental health problems. Life United are determined that no one else is ever left to suffer on their own and manager Hilton said: "One of the main reasons that this club has been set up is to raise awareness of men's mental health. We hope to create a team where we can grow and help players, supporters and everyone in between join together in the fight against mental health issues. One lingering issue/stereotype for men especially is that 'Men Don't Talk'. Our club hopes to work with local charities and organisations to eliminate that problem and create an environment where men can get help if needed and can have a set of ears to talk to.

"We want to be a club that is inclusive to all people; a place that people can fit in, be welcome and have a team to support together while doing this. One of the main benefits to combating against mental health is exercise. We are wanting to use our love of football to help fight against this. Mental health issues among men are the single biggest killer for ages under 45. As a club, we hold weekly talks before training to check in with each other and see how we are doing. We keep in touch during the week and have each others back too. The club has not been set up purely for football reasons; it has been set up to help anyone and everyone who may need it.

"We've helped each other move house, we've helped each other with job applications, with weekly shops when one of us might be struggling. What we are is a collective group of men who want to see each other succeed in life and get the help we need."

**Flat out:
Grandstand views
of Life United.**

Seeking help from above? Life's goalkeeper John Bigamore seeks divine intervention as his opponents celebrate.

20. DELIVERING A LESSON AT NEW SCHOOL VENUE

Saturday, April 24, 2.30pm
Clark Arena, Richmond School, Darlington Road
Richmond Town 5 Horden Community Welfare 4
Wearside League, Alan Hood Charity Cup

Plans for a big welcome party to celebrate Richmond's move to their new ground have had to be put on hold due to the Covid-19 crisis and the continuing ban on spectators. Their Wearside League games are being played behind closed doors, although that did not stop a couple of dozen hardy fans from the North Yorkshire town and their Horden visitors sneaking a peek at the new facilities through the fence from various grass banks outside.

The contrast between the new and old is stark. Town's Earls Orchard ground oozes character, on the banks of the River Swale beneath the imposing battlements of Richmond Castle in a delightful valley. The Clark Arena, is high on a hill, exposed to the wind, and is very 'functional' in appearance.

However, while the quaint town centre ground had the 'X factor' it had limited facilities and offered no scope for improvements to allow Town to climb the non-League pyramid. The new ground is currently little more than a MUGA (multi-use games area), accessed from the school's car park via a maze of winding paths. However, as well as a 4G surface, offering year-round training facilities, it also has floodlights, impressive changing rooms and a clubhouse. A stand should soon appear, although a shortage of hard-standing may prove problematic when the club decides to take a step up from the Wearside League.

The first-team made their debut at the new ground the previous week with a 3-2 last-gasp defeat to Durham Corinthians. Club secretary Jon Rutherford said it had been hard to judge a reaction to the new ground due to the lack of spectators. However, the players thought it was fantastic and the new facilities really are fabulous," he said.

"We've got six changing rooms so all 20-plus of our teams will be well catered for. We've got planning permission for a stand but the timescale on that depends on what happens with the restructure implications, as to the speed of progress."

Another big change at the club has been a new management team. Long-serving Neil Tarrant stepped aside for personal reasons and Jason Newall and Adam Emson have taken over as co-managers. Work commitments and a growing family meant it was impossible for Tarrant to devote as much time to the club as he wanted, although he will still to turn out for the over-40s.

Newall will continue to play. The dominant centre back was club captain and, now in his 30s, has played for the club right through the junior system, broken only by short spells in the Northern League with Shildon and Northallerton Town. Emson was a school mate of Newall but retired as a player following a freak head injury while on holiday a couple of years ago. The prolific striker, was lightning quick and played for Richmond as a youngster before moving on to a long Northern League career with Consett, Shildon, Bishop Auckland, Northallerton, Thornaby, Stokesley and Crook, before moving back to Richmond. His father Paul was a left-winger and scored 38 goals from 321 appearances in the Football League for Derby County, Grimsby Town, Wrexham and Darlington.

"Taking over was a surprise but I've played football all my life," said Emson. "Now I've got to an age where I've stopped so it was an obvious move. Jason is a club legend and has been here all his life. We went to school together so know each other really well and the Richmond football scene inside out. I loved playing at Earls Orchard. We got good crowds and always had a handful of groundhoppers because of its location but it wasn't great to play on. Once we get the stand put up here, it will look more like a football ground. We need our own identity and there's still a lot of work to do to make it look like a proper football ground.

"The training facilities here are incredible and it's a real hub for the town. It will enable us to move up the pyramid and keep the town's best young talent. In the past they've had to move away to progress. We've already got a few players in the first team who have progressed from the juniors."

That next generation of players were in action ahead of kick-off on a neighbouring pitch, while further down the hill behind the Clark Arena, Richmondshire CC's fourth XI were romping to a 133-run win over Preston on Tees in the North Yorkshire & South Durham Cricket League.

The benefit of having a hill-top location, is that there are long-range views over the cricket ground towards Catterick Racecourse and the Vale of Mowbray beyond. The downside is that even on a glorious sunny day, the strong wind blew bitterly cold until a half-time move to the shelter of a storage shed brought me the prize of a glorious sun trap. It also offered the bonus of eavesdropping on the match officials' pitch-side half-time deliberations – the good use of man management skills to get the best out of the players was perhaps expected; the durability of shorts and recent TV viewing less so.

The Clark Arena is a typical MUGA enclosure, fenced in with multi-use pitch markings and just one section for spectators, running three-quarters of the length of the near side. A high wall around one-and-a-half sides and a drop to the cricket ground behind the far goal means there is not much space between the pitch and fence for extending the viewing area. There are four floodlight towers either side of the pitch and a pair of dug-outs on the opposite side from the dressing room building, but only the home one was in use today with the visitors making their home on the near side.

The carpet-like pitch encouraged a passing game and both teams made the most of the superb surface to serve up a thrilling goal fest.

Twice the hosts opened a two-goal lead but Horden quickly reduced the gap and when they pulled it back to 4-4 in the 85th minute they were on a roll and there looked to be only one winner. Richmond thought otherwise!

The Alan Hood Charity Cup is being played to give teams some meaningful action after lockdown and Horden boasted a perfect record after beating Gateshead Leam Rangers 4-0 and Washington United 8-1. Richmond's only game had brought that 3-2 defeat to

Durham Corinthians but they made lightning start to try to give their new managerial pairing a win.

They served notice of their intentions after only five minutes when Adam Walker beat the offside trap for the first of many times as the Horden defence struggled to cope with the pace of the home attack and their swift inter-passing play. Goalkeeper Jamie Chappell was quick off his line to block on the edge of the area but was left helpless seven minutes later when a cross from the right saw Lee McCormack arrive at the head of a queue of players for a free header into the net. It was 2-0 after 28 minutes when Tom Kavanagh was toppled in the area, amid furious Horden cries of "he dived". Referee Tim Craig was unmoved by the protests and pointed to spot, from where home captain Kallumn Holbrook hammered home. Within a minute Horden were back in the game when Marc Moon tapped in from close range.

Walker's tricky play eventually brought a third goal for the hosts. Five minutes after the interval his shot was blocked at the expense of a flag kick and a short corner worked to perfection, despite home players voicing frustration at it not been crossed into area, when full-back James Mur ran forward to smash home the ball.

Richmond had no chance to consolidate that renewed two-goal advantage because after 54 minutes Hayden Pace was put through and held off defenders before tucking the ball into the net. Horden goalkeeper Chappell was becoming more of a sweeper as his porous defence struggled to master their offside trap and he was quick off the mark to block McCormack as he ran through one-on-one. However, it was 4-2 after 56 minutes when Holbrook stepped forward to strike his second of the game, this time from a free-kick on the edge the area. That gap lasted 16 minutes before Horden's Joe Bell converted an even more delicious free-kick into the top bin at the other end.

An awful pass from Richmond substitute Mark Lilley gave his opposite number Peter Crawford a free run into the area and he slotted home off the post to make it 4-4 in the 85th minute but the culprit soon made amends. Two minutes later Lilley got round the back of the Horden defence at a free-kick to fire in the winner amid more furious protests from Horden, this time claiming there had a been a foul on their own player before the one that led to the free-kick.

Co-manager Emson admitted he was relieved to see his team hang on for victory. "It was a crazy game," he said. "We'd not played for six months before last week's game and were struggling for fitness. We'd also been dropped in at the deep end as managers after Neil left. There had been no warning and it came out of the blue, but it was all amicable. I thought we more than deserved the win today but we struggled to kill them off. Twice we went two up and really needed to go three ahead to finish it. However, we've come on leaps and bounds since last week and I'm delighted with that."

Emson also revealed the team had played the whole game without a recognised goalkeeper. "We couldn't get a goalkeeper. Our first choice is a student and is in quarantine in Newcastle. The second choice is playing cricket and our back up has got family commitments with a young family and we weren't allowed to sign anyone this late in the season. In the end we played a midfielder in goal. Brandon Bishop had never played there before but his dad was a good keeper in his youth so it must have rubbed off. You wouldn't have known he wasn't a proper goalkeeper from the way he played though."

Emson was delighted to see his team go toe-to-toe with their opponents, recognising a failing of Richmond teams in the past. "Teams from here have always generally lacked match toughness against sides from the North East – it's probably a cultural thing; lads brought up in a nice little country market town are obviously a lot different to those from areas of Newcastle, Middlesbrough and Sunderland. We need more aggression, within the rules of the game obviously! We need to be more intimidating."

That new grit was definitely on show today!

Spot the difference: The backdrop at Richmond's new ground is a complete contrast to their old home (see chapter 13).

Comparing notes: Match officials at Richmond.

21. SING WHEN YOU'RE WINNING...

Tuesday, April 27
St Mary's Sports College, Cranbrooke Avenue, Hull
Sculcoates Amateurs 2 Hornsea Town 4
Humber Premier League

A footballer who honed his craft on the playing fields of Hull with a regular Perfect 10 went on to appear in front of sell-out crowds, won awards galore and played at some of the country's greatest venues... but he never appeared for England, or, for that matter, any professional club. Even so, it was always Happy Hour when his team jumped on the Caravan of Love.

Although Paul Heaton was an impressive and gritty centre back for a host of Saturday and Sunday league teams in and around the East Riding, it is as a singer he is better known, spending almost 700 weeks on the UK singles and album charts in a 36-year career.

Heaton was just starting to make a name for himself as part of the Housemartins when he was playing for Sculcoates in the East Riding County League and even when the big time beckoned, he remained a loyal player, even arranging gigs so that he could get back in time to make kick-off.

Although born on the Wirral and having lived in Sheffield and Surrey, Heaton spent 19 years in Hull and is glad to be regarded as a local lad made good from the city. He went on to more success with the Beautiful South and remains on many people's playlists with his latest songs alongside Jacqui Abbott.

For 18 of those years, Heaton turned out in the Hull Sunday League for one team, variously named Grandways, Mainbrace and Grafton Rangers, due to different sponsors and pub bases but the same set of lads.

"We rose from Division Five in 1984, out of the 21 divisions at the time, to Division One, just below the Premier, and stayed in that until I left Hull in 2001" said Heaton. "On a Saturday I began at Cherry Burton in Division One of the East Riding County

Division, playing three seasons there from 1984, and then was at Sculcoates for three seasons and finally at Cavalier. The last lot were a brilliant side, mainly made up of rogues from Orchard Park Estate but great footballers.

"I absolutely loved playing football in Hull. One great thing about it was that a lot of the real lads and tough nuts played rugby league on a Saturday and Sunday, which made the game a bit less aggressive and a bit more cultured. That's not to say there weren't rough teams – there were some very hard teams – but I never felt particularly threatened.

"As usual in local football, Saturday was more cultured than Sunday, and Sculcoates particularly had a really professional outlook for the time. I got taken down by a lad called Jeff Jones whose dad Trevor had starred for them back in the day. I loved the set-up because, as well as being serious, it was friendly too."

As Heaton's fame grew, he did come in for 'special' attention from opponents although on one occasion that was probably warranted. "I was in London doing the A Little Time video and it overran time wise and I needed to get back for an important Saturday semi-final with Sculcoates," recalled Heaton. "Eventually I said "look I've got to go, there's someone ill in Hull" and they wrote me out of the whole thing. I got back five minutes before kick-off and played. Ten minutes into the match one of the lads said 'What's that'? and I looked down to see my shirt was covered in sweat and brown make-up that I'd forgotten to take off after rushing from the video!

"I spent the rest of the first half frantically scrubbing my face and neck, determined that no-one else would notice that I'd turned up to an important match in make-up!"

However Heaton has no time for his fellow musicians with delusions of footballing grandeur, as he explained. "If there's one thing I dislike, it's pop stars who bleat on about having trials at such and such a club, or who would've made it if it wasn't for an injury, blah blah… I've never met a musician who's just played football, like me, at a half-decent level, their whole lives. Why? Because they have to have a glamorous story to everything they do, and the story of just playing every single Saturday and Sunday but never making the grade, doesn't sell records.

"Most musicians think buying a retro shirt and playing five-a side is a football career… If you look at The Beautiful South tours we frequently had southern gigs during the week and northern ones at the weekend, so that I could get back to play!"

Heaton has played more than 700 competitive matches at junior and amateur level and said: "I played competitive, 11-a side matches, from the age of nine – my debut was for the 36th Ranmoor Sheffield Cub Scouts – and carried on playing my whole life. I've got a record of them all and now have hundreds of shirts, badges, programmes, tickets and sticker collections," he said. "My house is a treasure trove of football."

Heaton still keeps in touch with many those old teammates and is happy to pop into his old locals for a natter. "Whenever I play a gig in the area, my old football team are usually there, so that's the main time I get to catch up on old times. We see a fair amount of each other and if I ever had a reunion, it wouldn't be for school or music, it would be the lads that I've played with down the years."

But will any of those old teammates get the chance to achieve their own moment of fame, alongside Heaton and current singing partner Abbott? The pair's Seven-inch Singles release was filmed in his old local, the Grafton in Hull, with a cast of regulars, while the I Don't See Them video was set just up the coast at Scarborough and the Loving Arms and Real Hope songs were accompanied by the Grimethorpe Colliery Brass Band in suitably evocative northern backdrops.

"I've always avoided embracing football too strongly but weirdly have written a couple of lyrics recently that have included football references," he said, so watch this space perhaps.

Heaton remains a regular football fan and said: "I still watch football at all levels and always have. If I was in the car with my dad and we passed a match, he'd pull over and we'd stand and watch, and talk to the people on the touchline for 15 minutes. The other Sunday I went with my youngest and my wife and walked to Hough End to watch half an hour of local football. On Wednesday I watched the whole of the Southern Combination League semi-final between Lancing and Lingfield, live online. I love junior football, women's football, love every glorious edition or version of the game. My dad was a coach and part-time scout and ran junior sides for his whole life. He introduced us to the foreign game and so we played in Germany, Holland and Belgium as youngsters. My brother is a qualified coach, his son plays semi-pro, and my other brother played to very good standard. We live and breathe football."

Another man who has lived and breathed football his whole life is Sculcoates secretary Tony Exton, who has been involved with the club for 60 years.

"Tony took it seriously and hated losing," recalled Heaton. "However, above all, he loved the game. When you carry that love for the game, you've got an immediate bond with others. That's why Tony and I got on.

"If I'd just turned up and couldn't play to a decent standard, Tony wouldn't be scared to tell me to sling me hook. The same if you had a poor game. But the thing I really liked about him was he always had a little glint in his eye. He was part Bobby Robson-part Northern stand-up comic. I'd also like to thank Tony for always treating me absolutely equally, without any bias, either against or in favour."

For Exton's part, he is proud of the part he played in Heaton's career and said: "Aye, he's done alright for himself but he was a half-decent midfield player when he was with us for a couple of seasons. He used to come on his bike and rope it up against a shed at the ground. ("I was a central defender with a midfielder's touch," corrected Heaton. "A bit small for that position but Gary Mabbutt and all that!)

"The Housemartins were just getting big at the time but he still turned out for us," added Exton. "He flew all the way back from Italy once for a game but it was so tight I daren't put him on and he wasn't best pleased! At one game we got changed in a caravan next to the pitch and the lads all started singing Caravan of Love, which he had in the charts at the time.

"He was a good lad and would join in all the social activities – he loved his beer and crisps! Paul was a real character and a great lad. I saw him out and about a few times after he'd made the big time and he was always up for a beer and chat. I saw him again six or seven years ago when I was on the train and we had a good catch up and chat."

Sculcoates have been one of the most successful sides in the Hull area for many years, since being formed for the 1946/1947 season. During that time they have had only two secretaries. Exton is currently keeping his eye on the paperwork in a role he took on "just to tide things over" following the death of the previous secretary – in 1972.

He celebrated his 82nd birthday a week after today's game but admits he was railroaded into joining the club and also had a shocking confession to make. "I joined in February 1961, almost by accident," he recalled. "I'd just done my National Service and arrived back at Paragon Station. I saw one of my old mates and he asked if I fancied going to watch Scully on Saturday as they had a few more of my mates playing for them. I said I've only just been demobbed and haven't been home for two years. Even so, I ended up going along. Of course they were short so I played. Don't tell anyone but I wasn't registered! I'm East Riding County League registration secretary now so that would be frowned on!"

Exton had served with the Yorkshire Regiment and, having never been further from Hull than Withernsea, found myself stationed in Germany, on guard duty at Spandau Prison, where Rudolf Hess and Albert Speer were kept.

"I'm back in barracks again now due to the Covid and my crutches," he said, although he is still actively involved in both the club and County League. "I still do the football because I like it and people are always ringing up for a chat, so it keeps my mind active. I've not been able to get to see a game for about four years. I'm struggling to walk and am on crutches. My mind is willing but my legs less so – my mouth is still going at full throttle though!"

Exton lists his proudest moments at the club as winning the County League five years on the bounce and three Senior Cups – a rare feat for an amateur club against the likes of Hull City, North Ferriby United and Bridlington Town. "We also represented the East Riding FA and won the Northern Counties Championship, beating Northumberland in the final at Ferriby. We were the first team to play as the county XI.

"We did talk about moving up in standard but the players were all happy playing with their mates on a Saturday and didn't fancy midweek treks to the other side of Yorkshire so we stayed where we knew. We also didn't have the facilities or money behind us. That might have meant we have lost a few players over the years but most of them came back when they realised what they were missing. "The contrast between us as amateurs and the likes of Brid Town in their hey days was highlighted when we played them in the Senior Cup, just before they won the FA Vase. We drew 2-2 and agreed to move the replay so it didn't clash with their Wembley preparations. They beat us 2-0 but after the game, while I was going round collecting the two quid subs from my players, their man was handing out hundreds of pounds in expenses to his lads."

Sculcoates originally played on playing fields at Oak Road before moving to the Hull & East Riding ground about 20 years go. "We've been plagued by flooding and once went six months without a home game. We decided to move to St Mary's to use the 3G there, to guarantee some games. Hopefully if we can get some grants and funding to sort out the drainage, we'll eventually move back to Hull & East Riding, which we still consider as 'home',"said Exton.

In their early days, Sculcoates used to travel to away games in an old camper van and he recalled home matches were also a bit of an adventure. "We had to clear the dog muck off the pitch before we could mark the lines with sawdust. The Humber Premier League has seen a great improvement in facilities but I don't really think the standard of play is a great deal different.

"There were some really rough pitches in the villages and it used to be a huge contrast when we'd play there one week and then be at Boothferry Park for the county cup final a few days later. When we played at the KC Stadium we were amazed at the dressing rooms. They were big enough to play five-a-side in!"

Going into this evening's match, I thought I'd got my possible report angles sorted well in advance of my trip to Hull. I knew the club were due to celebrate their 75th anniversary next year and that Exton had been there for the majority of that time, as well as the career of Heaton. Plenty of scope for tales there then… no need for much else?

However, who do I find giving the pre-match team talk but Hull City and Bradford City legend Dean Windass. Windass has joined Sculcoates as assistant to manager Tony Dobson and is enjoying being back at grassroots level, coaching the stars of tomorrow. He is also busy with a new building contracting venture, as well as enjoying life as a TV pundit and completing his second autobiography. That is sure to be an enlightening read, telling the tale of his colourful career and subsequent battle with alcohol and depression.

Windass said: "I'm concentrating on looking after the young kids after they've been released by pro clubs and there's a lot of great talent here."

That is a position Windass knows from bitter experience, having been released by Hull City at 16. He learned quickly and dusted himself down, battling back via Sunday League football and North Ferriby United before being re-signed by the Tigers and going on to a glittering career with teamss that included both Sheffield clubs, Middlesbrough and Aberdeen, chalking up nine seasons at the highest level of the British game alongside global superstars. Altogether he made more than 730 professional appearances, scoring almost 250 goals along the way.

A mix of problems saw him hit the headlines for all the wrong reasons after his retirement in 2010 at the age of 41 but he has worked hard to turn his life around and now puts together podcasts for mental health support.

"I've also been working from home via Zoom for Betfred match analysis, until the studio in Manchester is open again," added Windass.

Manager Dobson has known Windass since they were youngsters at Hull City together and said: "I was actually there when he was released. No one could believe how they'd let him go but at that time he was just another skinny 16-year-old. All credit to him for going away and building up his physique and going on to do what he has in the game. He's a great lad to have around and the players are in awe of him. He's giving so much back. His knowledge of the game is all there and the lads look up to him, hanging on his every word. They can only learn good things from him."

Windass spent the whole 90 minutes cajoling and encouraging his players and, despite the 4-2 defeat said: "It was pleasure to watch tonight. If we keep playing like that, we've got nothing to worry about."

The oldest player in the home line-up was Jack Rooks, at only 24, with several of his team-mates only 17 and 18 but they put on an entertaining show of quick-interpassing football, matched by their opponents in an encounter that would not have looked out of place several steps up the non-League ladder.

Sculcoates play in a 3G cage behind St Mary's Sports College's sports village, meaning an almost clinical atmosphere, especially with supporters not allowed. Those who had tried to sneak in to be pitch side were ejected ahead of kick-off, although the couple of dozen in attendance were free to watch through the open gate and wire mesh of the cage. The neighbouring pitch was hosting a PE session while, on the grass opposite, a local archery club was in full flight at the busy sports centre.

A first glance at the teams brought confusion with both appearing to be in all-black kits – thankfully the referee was in light blue! However, when they turned round, the hosts boasted a chequerboard pattern on the front of their shirts, while Hornsea had fluorescent green fronts; very similar to their goalkeeper's lime green shirt!

The kit clash obviously threw the hosts because they allowed free rein to Adam Gibson to open the scoring after only five minutes. It was all square after 20 minutes when Ben Flowerdew cut in from the left wing and curled a superb shot into the opposite top corner of the net.

The two sides looked evenly matched, despite Hornsea struggling at the wrong end of the table after losing eight of their previous 11 fixtures, including 11-2 and 8-2 tonkings by leaders Beverley Town and Hedon Rangers respectively. Scully were sitting comfortable in mid-table with a 4-4-4 record and had the psychological advantage of a 4-0 cup win at Hornsea earlier in the campaign.

Defences were on top to stifle the creative midfield and attacking play but home goalkeeper Cal Barrett had to be alert to parry a long-range effort from Connor Binney and was grateful to his guardian defenders for a hurried clearance. On the stroke of half-time Barrett was tested again, scrambling to his right to push Hornsea left back Ben Leyland's 25-yard shot round a post at full stretch.

An end-to-end encounter soon saw Hornsea on the attack with right back Kieran Baines pulling the ball across the face of goal and through the finger and legs of Barrett, only for it to be hacked off the line by a covering defender as several of the Seasiders' forwards lurked. An intricate short corner routine from Hornsea after 58 minutes was wasted when they overplayed things but they got it spot on two minutes later when another corner was floated to the far post for Leyland to crash home a header.

Tom Attwood then slammed the ball into the side netting after outpacing the home defence and drawing the goalkeeper. Flowerdew twisted and turned his way into the Hornsea area soon after but his shot was well saved by Lewis Ashton. The equaliser came after 68 minutes with Flowerdew again the provider, this time finishing off a teasing run with a cross from the goalline for Aris Cunha to convert from close range.

Hornsea needed only two more minutes to regain the lead when Attwood made up for his earlier miss with a shot high into the net. Cunha then burst through the visiting defence but his hard-driven cross was too heavy for his teammates to convert as they lunged at full stretch in vain.

With Sculcoates pushing hard for another equaliser, they were caught on the break in the second minute of stoppage time when Lewis Reeves forced the ball in from a corner to complete the scoring.

The average age of the Sculcoates team tonight was barely 20 but a week earlier it was significantly higher, thanks to the role played by Dobson. The 56-year-old manager turned out in the black and white of Scully for the first time in 39 years; a long career with the likes of Goole Town and North Ferriby United the meat in his Sculcoates sandwich.

"I didn't expect to be playing again but had to make up the numbers until some more of the lads who were late arrived," said Dobson, who this evening was keeping fit by running the line. My knees knew about it the following day, even though I do keep myself fairly fit," he added ruefully

Dobson is the latest in a long line of managers who have previously played for the club, including Mark Lever, who was there as a teenager before being snapped up by Grimsby Town and embarking on a 15-year professional career, which also included Bristol City and Mansfield Town.

Dobson followed him into the hot seat and set about rebuilding the team with a focus on youth. "Most of the players have been with me for 11 or 12 years," he said. "We all started together at Hessle Sporting and then moved to Hall Road Rangers Reserves. From there we came en bloc to Sculcoates."

Dobson thought his team had played their part in an enthralling game and hope they had done enough to earn a share of the points. "We've played worse than that and won games," he said. "They created more chances and took them, we didn't. That was the difference. I thought 3-2 was about fair but they caught us pushing for the equaliser but it was a very attractive game to watch."

Another long-serving member of the off-field team at Scully is chairman Steve Burrluck, who has been at club since joining as a player 32 years ago. "We try to run the club to a semi-professional standard, even though we are strictly amateur," he said. "We've got all the right gear but training has been hard for the last 12 months or so due to Covid.

Burrluck said the proudest moment of his lengthy career with the club has been the Northern Counties Cup win. "It was a tremendous honour and a great trophy to see but it only saw the light of day three times in the year we had it," he said. When we were presented it with it we were told to make sure it was insured because it was silver plated and worth £25K. We brought it out for a clubman dinner and then we saw it again when we handed it back. That was it! The rest of the time it was under lock and key."

One of many Sculcoates treasures!

On the ball Paul: Paul Heaton in action during his Hull days in the 1980s.

Hard graft: Paul Heaton (front row, third from right) with his Grafton teammates.
Pictures: courtesy of Paul Heaton.

Temporary role: Tony Exton agreed to step in for a short time as Sculcoates' secretary almost half a century ago!

A tiger in the tank: Dean Windass passes on advice.

22. A REAL FIELD OF BATTLE

Saturday, May 1, 2021
Wales High School, Kiveton
Kiveton Park 2 Penistone Church Reserves 1
Sheffield & Hallamshire County Senior League Cup

It was a lovely day for an afternoon in Wales, despite not finishing work until 2pm and with a kick-off time of 3pm. No, I don't boast a private jet or time travel machine… I was simply planning to go watch Kiveton Park at their new ground in the village of Wales, near Rotherham. It is the home of the 'Father of Modern Football' – Herbert Chapman.

However, he is only one member of the family of footballers passing through Kiveton on their way to greater things. Club history researcher Lee Hicklin has been overwhelmed with the rich seam of famous players connected to the club he has discovered. "There's been lots of players from Kiveton who have gone into the professional game," said Hicklin. "So many in fact that the Empire News in 1940 said that, pro rata, the village had turned out more professional football players than anywhere in England, apart from the Shropshire town of Oakengates."

Among those players has been, arguably the game's greatest innovator and manager, Chapman. He led both Huddersfield Town and Arsenal to a string of Football League and FA Cup triumphs and was also responsible for many of today's tactics – the use of physiotherapists and the introduction of numbered shirts, as well as championing floodlights and European club competitions.

The Kiveton Park hall of fame includes more than 20 other players who made it in the professional game, among them Birmingham City legend Walter Wigmore, Sheffield Wednesday FA Cup winner Harry Chapman (brother of Herbert), England international Herbert Morley, of Grimsby Town and Notts County, Manchester United title winner Leslie Hofton, Chelsea's Eric Oakton and, more recently, York City fans' hero Wayne Hall and Scarborough Football League promotion-winner Alan Kamara.

One explanation for the club's home settlement's unusual name comes from the word Waelas, meaning 'field of battle', and that was certainly the case in today's clash with Penistone Church Reserves. A blood and thunder encounter saw the visitors twice reduced to nine men, following a sin-binning and two sendings off as they belied their suffix with a far-from Christian approach to the beautiful game. A late penalty equaliser and even later winner for the home team made this an encounter to savour for the small group of spectators in attendance.

Penistone whinged and whined their way through the second half with a series of robust challenges ensuring referee Harry Lever was kept on his toes. Kiveton Park gave as good as they got in combat but held their tongues better and, despite having a minority share of possession and chances, pulled off an unexpected victory against opponents from one division higher.

The first half proved to be largely uneventful after Alex Thompson had given Kiveton a 17th-minute lead, when he reacted sharply to Brad Davies' belting effort, which hammered against a post, converting the rebound before the groans of dismay had left his teammates' throats. Soon after, Mitch Savage found space in the corner of the penalty area but his full-blooded shot was tipped round by Jonathan Parker. Penistone's coaching team obviously delivered a rocket up their charges' backsides at half-time as the visitors swarmed forward after the break.

However, several players were too fired up and Penistone No.9, Brad Kemp, soon took centre stage as complainer in chief – berating all and sundry; opponents, teammates and referee alike. It was no surprise when he was sent to the bench for a 10-minute cooling-off period after one outburst too many. That heralded a string of robust challenges and players from both teams surrounding beleaguered referee Lever demanding action. Penistone then started to take things further, dishing out retribution of their own, resulting in two red cards.

After 68 minutes Tim Council was booked for kicking hell out of the back of his team's dug-out after being substituted and two minutes later his colleague George Ellis was also shown the yellow card for a late lunge on Parker. That failed to cool things and within three minutes Ellis was booked again for another ill-judged challenge after tackles flew in wildly from both teams. His subsequent red card reduced the visitors to nine men. Kemp returned to the action a minute before his 10 minutes were up but had missed barely five minutes of the action.

It was all square after 80 minutes when Church's Lewis Dickinson was felled in the penalty area, sparking the turn of the home team to surround Mr Lever in protest. Jack Moore waited his time and held his nerve to slot the ball to the opposite side of the goalkeeper's dive. Two minutes later Penistone were back down to nine men when Charlie Shepherd was dismissed for lashing out after a series of lunging challenges from both teams. With five minutes to go, Kiveton got the winner. A shot across the face of goal found Thompson at the back post to ram in his second of the game.

Mr Lever had soon had enough and brought the game to a conclusion after just two minutes of stoppage time. For Kiveton club volunteer Hicklin, it was pay back time. The club historian said: "They beat us in the Sheffield Association Cup semi-final two years ago when they got a last-minute winner after we had two men sent off."

Historian is just one of Hicklin's roles at the club. He is also groundsman and programme editor but said the small team of volunteers who ran things at the club were all multi-tasking with a string of jobs between them. "I know every club relies on volunteer help but we are lucky here in that many of us are still the right side of 50," he said, pointing to how many similar clubs had folded when their committee and helpers had retired or passed away, with no younger blood to replace them. That augurs well for Kiveton Park, whose future is secure after a few nail-biting years when they were just surviving at their former Hard Lane ground.

It had been home to the club since they were formed in 1881 and was a miners welfare ground. However, it did not meet the criteria for the club to stay in the Northern Counties East League, with limited facilities and no floodlights, despite having attracted decent crowds during their Yorkshire League days from the 1960s onwards.

Hicklin explained: "The club was growing so much, with so many junior teams coming on board but the ground owners were not very forward thinking and the club felt as if it was being stifled. It was a typical miners welfare ground, with a great stand but only two men's teams playing there. We had to rebuild the dug-outs two or three times in the years before we left, due to vandalism and we had to do something major to move forward."

That came with a switch to their new ground on the playing fields at Wales High School. Situated at the end of Storth Lane, opposite the school, with a small 'school staff only' compound and on-street parking, it offers only basic facilities at the moment but is changing as the club grows.

"At Hard Lane we could only have two teams but here we've got more than 20, including juniors at all age ranges and two for women," said Hicklin. "There are eight pitches, including two full-size ones."

The main pitch has a string and post surround, with no hard-standing. A selection of portable buildings along the near side house a cafe, clubhouse, toilet block and changing rooms, with dugouts on the opposite side of the pitch. The club produces an excellent match programme, available for just £1 from the cafe. As well as the usual hot drinks, cold beverages and confectionery, crisps, etc, they also do a great line in bacon and sausage sandwiches and home-baked cakes, including flapjack that my wife rated as "excellent" when I got home with her surprise present from the match. Not the usual gift from the club shop!

Across the village at Hard Lane, the ground still has its main stand and Hicklin admitted their old home probably still looks a better ground than the new one but there's no scope to improve it. "We've got plans to move things forward here," he said. "We have a 25-year lease and the school are fully on board as partners. We've already got a clubhouse and have built a beer garden behind it. We're moving the main pitch towards the entrance this summer to make way for a 3G pitch.

"For the last two seasons we've been pushing for promotion to the Premier Division but Covid has stopped us. From there, we'd be able to get back into the Northern Counties East League eventually. It shouldn't be a problem getting floodlights and a stand here but that's all in the future and we have no time scale for that."

Hicklin is busy working on a history book of the club and had hoped to release it this November to tie in with the club's 140th anniversary, however, it is proving to be taking longer than expected. That is partly down to the amazing research he has gathered, showing that the club is 11 years older than originally thought. "Our formation year had always been thought to be 1892 but I discovered football was being played in the village in 1877," said Hicklin, who has spent countless hours at libraries in Worksop, Rotherham and Sheffield, digging out the club's history. The present club must have been formed in 1881 because it was registered at the Sheffield FA in 1883 and you had to have been going for two years to be accepted into that.

"Other than the wars and a couple of season in the 1990s when we just ran as a Sunday side, we've been playing all that time.

"I've put a lot of effort into researching the club's history. I've always loved history and football is doing both together has been a pleasure. I'm happy I've done as much research as I can and it's just a case of writing it all up now. I've got as far as the 1980s but I must admit I enjoyed the research more! The hardest part was when we were in the Worksop League in the 1950s and reports and results were few and far between. For many seasons there were only occasional tables and big cup match reports in the papers. We've now got a complete record of games since we joined the Yorkshire League in 1963."

Tucking in: Picnic time in Wales.

Net gains: Historian Lee Hicklin gets some help with his after-match duties at Kiveton

23. A BERRY NICE WAY TO THUNDER INTO THE FINAL

Tuesday, May 11, 2021
Berry Brow Rec, Ladyhouse Lane
Berry Brow 2 Linthwaite Athletic 1
Huddersfield League Barlow Cup, semi-final

Thundery weather matched an equally stormy encounter as these two teams went at it hammer and tongs for a place in the Barlow Cup final. Holders Linthwaite just about shaded possession but it was the hosts who proved more clinical in front of goal and grew stronger as the game progressed to earn a long-awaited victory over their near neighbours in front of a vociferous crowd.

Referee Ian Daffern and his assistants Dwayne Chappell and Joe Wink-Simmonds were kept busy with tackles flying in and temperatures reaching boiling point as forks of lightning flickered around the surrounding hills. Despite the often wince-inducing clashes, both teams managed to keep all 11 of their players on the pitch, although Daffern did have to make use of his yellow card frequently.

With no restriction on spectator numbers, thanks to the village recreation ground being an open space, around 250 fans lined the touchlines. The hosts held a slight numerical advantage there but it was the visiting fans, from all of four miles away, who won in the volume stakes. Bizarrely, Covid-19 regulations mean that clubs with an enclosed ground, who could enforce admission numbers and social distancing, are banned from allowing fans in, while those like tonight, playing on public grounds, are immune as they have no control over how many watch or how they behave.

Home manager Liam Walton was predicting a tight encounter between the teams who were lying first and second in the Huddersfield League Division One table before a coronavirus-induced shutdown in December. "They're a good side and will be a tough test for us but we're good as well," he said. "It's the hardest draw we could have got but you've got to beat the best to win anything. It should be a cracking game. They're still the holders. They won it in 2018/19 and last season's competition was abandoned due to Covid."

The Barlow Cup is normally a knockout competition for teams in the top two divisions but is being played in group stages this season, with the winners of four six-team groups meeting in the semi-finals. Berry Brow had recorded four wins from four, plus a walkover at Honley, to book their place in the last four, while Linthwaite matched that, apart from having a walkover recorded against them, when they had been due to play Dalton Dynamos. The night's other semi-final would see Newsome win 3-2 at Scholes, with the final due to be played at Golcar United later in the month.

It is one of three semi-finals Berry Brow are involved in. The reserves are in the last four of the Richardson Cup, while the A and B teams meet for a place in the Gee Cup final.

Linthwaite were keen to hang on to the trophy and created the first good chance after 11 minutes when a shot from the edge of the area crashed against the woodwork with home goalkeeper Luke Haigh helpless. Eight minutes later a Berry Brow corner was cleared off the goal line and Ben Dobson fired the loose ball into the side netting. The first argy bargy erupted after 25 minutes, resulting in the first booking of the night for a home player, followed by an equalising caution for Linthwaite when more handbags were swung four minutes later.

In between those flashpoints, Berry Brow should have gone ahead when two players found themselves in front of a gaping goal from a corner but the ball somehow screwed off one of their heads and over from practically on the goalline. Linthwaite had looked the more likely to score as they pushed forward in numbers but it was the hosts who took the lead after 41 minutes. A free-kick proved too hot to handle for Linthwaite goalkeeper Josh Ankers and, before he could grab hold of the ricochet, Wayne Shooter stooped to head in. Two minutes later the home team had Haigh to thank for a good save at the foot of a post when Ryan Wadsworth curled a free-kick superbly over the defensive wall and towards the bottom corner of the net.

Distant thunder grew louder and the heavens had opened by the time the second half got under way but the downpour failed to douse the passions of the two teams. Berry Brow were desperate to get their first win over Linthwaite since their Division Two title-winning season five years ago but were made to step up a gear after the visitors pulled level. Seven minutes after the interval, Connor Beaumont beat the home offside trap and chipped a delightful shot over Haigh, watching it drop just inside the far post before being engulfed by delighted team mates.

Parity lasted only 14 minutes before Berry Brow struck what proved to be the winner when centre back Richard Oakley rose highest to head in from a corner. Haigh pulled off a good save to keep out another dipping free-kick from Wadsworth after 76 minutes and soon after Joe Brennan was denied at the other end by an equally excellent block from Ankers before a couple of home efforts tested only the alertness of the horses grazing on the hillside behind Ankers' goal.

The final whistle provoked short celebrations from the home players and supporters before attention was quickly shifted to taking down the nets and seeking respite from the rain in their new dressing room block. For the visitors it was a case of a dash back to their cars for shelter as Covid regulations do mean they cannot share the facilities, even on a public playing field...

Had they been able to visit those changing rooms, they would have been privy to a remarkable story. Long-standing committee member Neil Atkinson said: "Before we got the new changing rooms we had nothing. From 1963 we used a shed in the Methodist Church grounds for about 15 years. From there we moved to Berry Brow Liberal Club and converted the under-dwelling there (the building is built into a hillside), which meant a 3-400 yard walk for the players.

"When we were putting in the new changing rooms here, we used the local cricket club at Armitage Bridge for two or three years, while we raised the funds to finish work here."

The club worked hard to raise the funds to convert an old steel shipping container into suitable changing rooms and Atkinson said: "One of our guys is a civil engineer and had a container going spare; it was just a metal box really. We raised £30,000, including lots from all the players, as well as grants from the Football Foundation, The Premier League and FA Facilities Fund Small Grants Scheme and the Skipton Building Society. The insides were all fitted out professionally and include changing rooms for two teams and the match officials, as well as showers."

Some of that money had a loose connection to some of football's mega-stars. Berry Brow A team's occasional goalkeeper Simon Mooney is a professional photographer and film maker. He is more used to mixing with the game's elite – David Beckham, Wayne Rooney, Steven Gerrard and players from the England national team, Everton and Spurs have been among those regularly in his focus. His clients include Audi, Umbro, Sony, Fiat and McDonald's.

However, this time he pointed his camera in the direction of his teammates for a fundraising Calendar Girls-style production to help towards the cost of the changing rooms. The semi-naked dressing room shots of his teammates proved a winning combination. Mooney told the Huddersfield Examiner at the time: "I have done these kind of shoots before and sometimes you don't realise you have captured someone completely naked, so you have to be discreet and be careful when you are editing, as not everyone has a finely-honed physique! We don't want to embarrass anyone."

Atkinson said the project had been Mooney's idea and had gone down well with most of the players. "A few were begging for him to use Photoshop to help them out though," he recalled.

Manager Walton said the club was continuing to evolve and improve their facilities. "Our next plans are to extend the changing rooms then have a look at improving the pitch."

However, there are no plans to play any higher in the football pyramid. "A lot of our lads like playing here, being with their mates and not having to travel too far for games," said Walton. "They're all mates and want to play together at a level where they can still have a laugh together."

Atkinson agreed with that and added: "We just want to make the facilities as good as possible for the community. Apart from a couple of new lads this season, the teams has been together for years. We usually only get three men and a dog to watch us but we are getting more and, as you can see, there's plenty down tonight."

Berry Brow were founded in 1899 as Berry Brow Wesleyans, with links to a local church, and played in Birch Road. In 1921 the village's other Methodist church formed a team, called Berry Brow Salem, and the two were keen rivals for years before merging in 1936. That team played on until 1961 when they folded but it was just two years later that Berry Brow were reborn and continue to this day.

Atkinson said: "Some youngsters in the village started it up again in 1963 with one team and we're still going but with four teams now. We've always played in the Huddersfield League but did have a team in the Huddersfield Works & Combination League for 20 years until the league folded. All four teams are now in the same competition, one in each division. All our teams are adult ones. We don't have a junior section but do get youngsters coming through from Netherton, who have a big junior set-up. We've had quite few players for there in the past, especially when Mark Dobson was involved. He's sadly deceased now but was involved with both clubs and encouraged the youngsters from there to come to us when they got to 16-or-so.

"With four teams, we have to use two other grounds, so they can all play. This is our main one but we've also got one a couple of villages away at Farnley Tyas, which we've used for about 20 years, and another at Crosland Moor.

Berry Brow's Rec ground is hard to see from the road, hidden on a plateau. It has a large grass bank on one side, with a railway line and trees on the other with a backdrop of horses on the hillside behind the far goal. The changing room block is at the foot of the hill next to the road.

Berry Brow is situated at the top of the Holme Valley road. It twists and turns its way up through shady woodland with the occasional glimpse of the river Holme far below to reveal at journey's end – a pair of high-rise flats! Apart from that bizarre blot on the landscape, the village is picturesque and something of a hidden treasure.

From my home, it should be a straight-forward journey – simply head west and aim for the twin masts on Emley Moor. However, my satnav always adjusts to take the same route, no matter how hard I try to ignore it and go straight across – I always end up going south west and then north. For reasons best known to itself, the satnav decided the return journey had to be even longer, via the M62 and A1. Again I tried to override it but ended up stuck in Huddersfield's one-way system and roadworks before getting caught up in the torrential downpour that had passed over Berry Brow earlier in the evening.

Above - Standing room only: A big crowd for the Barlow Cup semi-final at Berry Brow.

Right - Horse play: Interested spectators at Berry Brow.

24. OLD BOYS ARE ON TOP

Saturday, May 15, 2021
Marine Villa Road, Knottingley
Kellingley Welfare 1 Old Centralians 2
West Yorkshire League, Division Two Cup

How Kellingley could have done with the input of their most experienced player today after losing their way in the second half. Veteran Phil Sutton was left on the touchline, shrugging off the heavy downpour, not even listed on the home team sheet.

He wasn't injured and not suspended, however, the fact he is 72 this year might have swayed the management's decision, although it is only seven years since he last turned out for the first team.

"I sign on as a player every year, just in case," said Sutton, who arrived at the ground bearing a fold-up chair and golf umbrella, fully prepared for the forecast rain and fresh from refereeing a match that morning.

"You never know when I might be needed and that was the case in my last game. We were short, funnily enough at Old Centralians, and I came on for 20 minutes-or-so, even though I was 65 at the time. When I signed on this season we got a call from the league registration secretary asking if we'd misprinted my year of birth but, no, it's definitely 1949!

"I must admit I also played another game just before that but was a 'ringer'. We needed a goalkeeper to play in a cup match but he hadn't played a league match to qualify so I played under his name the week before at Ilkley. The referee knew me but somehow we got away with it."

That little 'oversight' did not blemish Sutton's 56-year record at the club, for which he has received an FA award to honour his 50 years service to football. Sutton first signed for the club in their debut season, way back in 1965 when they joined the Castleford & District Sunday League. Since then the progress has been made via the Bentley and Selby Leagues to the West Yorkshire League and he has been there all the way in a variety of roles.

Most Yorkshire mining teams have a long and proud history so it comes as something of a surprise to discover that although Kellingley have the pride, they are relative babes in arms in pit terms. The shafts at Kellingley Colliery were not sunk until 1960, with coal being produced from April 1965.

As in previous generations, the discovery of coal brought a huge influx of miners from across the UK and at its peak 2,000 men were employed there. The opening coincided with the closure of many pits in Scotland and it was no surprise when a football team soon sprang up. Other immigrants came from Wales, Cumberland and the North East, housed in the Warwick Estate in Knottingley.

However, within a short 20 years, pits across Yorkshire were closing, accelerated in the mid-1980s under Margaret Thatcher's Government. Kellingley survived, as the largest deep-mine in Europe, eventually closing in December 2015. Now the 151-acre former colliery site is being transformed into a new development called Konect, which will offer 1.45 million square feet of manufacturing and distribution space, with hundreds of new jobs coming in over the next decade.

One area of the complex not being swallowed up by development is the football ground in Marine Villa Road, home of 'The Kells', more officially known as the Kellingley Welfare Junior Football Club.

Children had been playing sports on Green House Fields since 1938, when it was decided that a large recreational area was needed for the growing population in the area. The Kellingley (Knottingley) Social Centre was built with a youth club and bowling alley attached. Facilities including a sports centre, swimming pool, library, bowls green and tennis courts were added to cater for the miners and their families, including a grandstand at the football ground, which the club have since had refurbished.

"We used to have a lot of miners play for us and were nicknamed the Pitmen," said Sutton. "They all came to the social club and it would be heaving on a Saturday and Sunday, I could take £90 on a raffle every week. They lived on the Warwick Estate and a new club was built there – the SYD Club (Scottish, Yorkshire and Durham) marking where the men had come from.

The club started as one for youngsters and Sutton recalled: "A leader at the youth club was an ex-pro and thought it would be a good idea to start up a team for the 16 and 17 year old lads there. In 1967 the team coach booked nine of us players to go on a coaching week at the England World Cup training camp at Lilleshall. There was a group of eight lads from Liverpool and eight from Aston Villa, as well as us. We spent the whole week being coached by the England coaches. It was the best week of my life – all we did was eat, sleep and play football."

That inspired the club to enter a team in the Castleford Sunday League as a transition to adult football and Sutton said: "Games were played on Sunday afternoons in those days but they had to switch to Sunday mornings after they found out how hard it was to get players out of the pubs to play in the afternoon!

"We had a short spell in the West Yorkshire League before joining the Bentley & District League where we had quite a bit of success.

"In the 1990s we added a second team and joined the Selby League. We did well and both teams kept winning their divisions. Unfortunately, two teams from the same club couldn't play in the same division, so the reserves couldn't be promoted. In our third season in the league we were told we had to change it to an A and a B team and then things got complicated because players had to be transferred from one to the other if they wanted to pay with their mates. In our first season as two clubs, we finished first and third in the league."

The Kells wanted to test themselves against better teams but could not get back into the West Yorkshire League because the pitch was not railed off. "Then we had a stroke of luck, and a little bit of opportunism," said Sutton. "Ferrybridge Amateurs had to remove their pitch surround because it was too close to the pitch and was dangerous. The council took it down and put it into their storage yard, which just so happened to back on to our ground. We saw it and asked if we could have it.

The council said yes, but we had to install it and, luckily, got some more from a local scaffolding company. A player had a company that helped put the railings up and we got it done in a couple of days. "That meant we were able to return to the West

Yorkshire League, where we've been ever since, although it's been a bit up and down."

That was certainly the case a decade ago when current Boston United manager Craig Elliott left his first position in management. "We nearly folded when he left us in the lurch," said Sutton.

Elliott had enjoyed a tremendously successful year at Kellingley, winning a league and cup treble. He arranged to form a second team of 16 and 17 year old lads to play in the Selby League and put together a good team for the forthcoming West Yorkshire Premier Division season, However, just before the season started, he upped and left to take over at Glasshoughton, taking six or seven key players with him.

"It left us in limbo and we had to think long and hard about whether to pull out of the West Yorkshire League and start again in the Selby League," said Sutton. "In the end we decided to stick at it and withdrew our Selby League application. We'd worked hard to get Charter Standard and were one of the first clubs round her to get it so had to do the best we could."

Consecutive relegations followed and, apart from one season in Division One, the Kells have been in Division Two ever since.

"We were hopeful of promotion last season but lockdown put an end to that," added Sutton. "We've got no ambition to go higher now but we do often talk about getting floodlights and hard-standing. We did apply to BT when they were funding floodlight systems for teams in return for the use of them as mobile phone masts but were unsuccessful. We could apply for grants but our lease with the council runs out in 2025 so we can't meet the minimum tenure demands."

Things had looked good for Kellingley at half-time today; a goal to the good and always threatening to score thanks to some dominant wing play. However, the second half was a different story with Old Centralians hitting back and even a missed penalty did not dent their winning challenge.

A reminder that football is only a game was given in stark fashion before kick-off with a minute's silence to remember nine-year-old Jordan Banks, who had been killed by a lightning strike in Blackpool earlier in the week while out training.

The teams tested each other out in the opening stages with the hosts' patient passing game in contrast to Old Centralians counter-attacking style. The first good chance came after 14 minutes when Brandon Cummings' looping header left the Leeds side's goalkeeper Joe Royce wrong footed but the ball dropped just the wrong side of the cross bar. Two minutes later Royce was again left as a spectator when a loose ball 35 yards out was picked up by home captain Evan Tyson. He took it in his stride and launched a cracker towards goal, crashing past Royce but hammering off a post and across the face of goal.

A heavy rain shower arrived midway through the first half, forcing all but two of the 70-strong crowd scuttling for cover in the stand or under trees behind the goal. That left just the two management teams and hardy spectators Sutton and his pal Mick on the touchline as the heavens opened.

An absorbing encounter ensured fans' focus remained on the game rather than the conditions and a partisan home crowd, led by one vocal fan resplendent in blue and yellow wig, brought a bit of big-match atmosphere with their chants echoing round the back of the stand.

The stand, built on top of the changing room block, consists of nine steps of steep terracing but only the rearmost offered respite from the rain, although the top step came with the handicap of a low roof – as I found out to my cost later.

Meanwhile, on the pitch, Dylan Hutchinson's shot was saved by Royce and the loose ball was hacked away from inside the six-yard box by Jack Calvert just as Cummings pulled the trigger to tap into an open net. The impressive Jordan Hutchinson's tricky run from midfield into the penalty area looked to herald the opening goal but the ball ran away from him after he beat a fourth defender, allowing Royce to dash out and collect. After 35 minutes Cummings' corner picked out Tyson at the far post but he powered a header narrowly wide.

The deadlock was broken two minutes later when Kellingley broke from a rare visitors' attack and Jordan Hutchinson galloped clear before laying the ball into the path of Regan Fish to smash it into the roof of the net to earn a half-time lead.

Old Centralians were formed in 1925 when former pupils from the Leeds Central High School started a team. After merging with Thoresby High School to form City of Leeds School, now Leeds City Academy, they were among the founder members of the Yorkshire Old Boys League (now the Yorkshire Amateur League). After many years of success the first team moved up to the West Yorkshire League earlier this century.

It was the old boys who handed out a footballing lesson in the second half with Kellingley's dangerous wingmen starved of the ball as the visitors picked up the pace. After 50 minutes a shot was blocked and the loose ball fell for Matt O'Keefe in front of a yawning net but his goalbound effort brought the save of the match from Josh Wright, throwing himself to his right to turn the point-blank effort round a post.

Old Centralians were given the chance of pulling level on the hour mark when Kris Sleight fouled Jones and referee Alan Clough pointed straight to the spot. Luke Harrop stepped up but Wright guessed right and saved low to his right. However, an away goal always looked likely and it came with 14 minutes left to play when Royce's goal kick was flicked on for O'Keefe to fire in the equaliser. The winner came in the 85th minute. A free-kick was delivered into the heart of the home goalmouth and O'Keefe was on hand to head in his second goal. Rothery had the chance to make the points secure in the last minute when he was left in acres of space but his shot was turned round a post by the hard-working Wright.

Top - Soaking up the action: Long-serving Phil Sutton, right, was among the hardy spectators at Kellingley

Above - Taking shelter: Fans pack into the stand at Marina Villa Road.

Left - It's coming home: Kellingley's 1967 Lilleshall squad

25. A FAN-TASTIC RETURN TO ACTION

Wednesday, May 19, 2021
DSM Memorial Ground, Church View Road, Penistone
Penistone Church 5 Wakefield AFC 1
Yorkshire Trophy

They are sounds that have been missing for months and the welcome return of fans brought with it rounds of applause, cheers, groans and all the usual atmosphere that Covid-19 has robbed us of in recent months.

The fact those fans were treated to six goals and a plethora of missed chances only served to heighten the excitement as Penistone welcomed the Yorkshire Trophy to the DSM Memorial Ground with open arms. They had lost their opening match in the competition 1-0 at Brighouse on Monday and looked to be in danger of another defeat when their visitors from the Sheffield County Senior League took the game by the throat in the early stages, forcing a string of corners to put pressure on the hosts. However, slowly but surely the hosts gained a foothold and by the end of the night were worthy winners.

The teams took time to work each other out and chances were at a premium until the game burst into life just after the half-hour mark. The only chance of note before that saw Jed Wilkinson's cross deceive home goalkeeper Chris Snaith and bounce off the bar before being headed away after 23 minutes.

Four minutes later Nicky Guest and John Pugh both fired warnings of the approaching storm with two long-range testers for Wakefield goalkeeper Alessio Ruch, which he saved comfortably. After 29 minutes Kurtis Turner cut in from the touchline and his shot was pushed away by Ruch into the path of Brett Lovell. He slammed it into the net but had seen the linesman's flag go up for offside before he had chance to celebrate.

The opening goal came after 33 minutes when Wakefield left back Corey Woodward clattered into Guest, leaving referee

Gareth Thomas an easy decision to award a penalty, which Kieran Ryan fired home.

It was a simple task for Thomas but for watching Penistone president Keith Hackett, it brought back memories of his early refereeing days. Hackett's career included 23 years at professional level, taking in the FA Cup final, FA Charity Shield, European Championship Finals and Olympic Games, as well as the Premier League.

Now 76, he has been a regular visitor to Penistone since his teenage years and now eschews the professional game to rekindle his grassroots passion, watching most of the club's games, home and away.

"I was officiating at about 100 games a season at my peak," recalled Hackett. "That included local Sunday games and one week I remember refereeing a European Championship game between West Germany and Italy on the Wednesday and the following weekend was doing the Black Bull Taverners against the Angel pub. No matter what the level, I'm just the referee.

"One game I remember well was in the early days of Sunday football at Catcliffe. When I turned up there were no lines and the goalposts were beer barrels! I asked how we'd know if the ball had gone in and the players said it's up to you – we'll go by whatever decision you make – and they did! Another problem was when I gave a penalty. I had to stride out the distance and make a mark with my foot because there was no penalty spot."

However, back to tonight and Hackett will have admired the next goal, even though it came from the opposition. Just three minutes after Penistone had gone ahead, Wakefield were level when Harley Blankley lashed home a shot from the edge of the area that flew into the top corner of Snaith's goal.

Cheers from Wakefield's fans had barely died down when they were behind again just a minute later. This time Ryan pulled the ball back for Jordan Coduri to score.

The see-saw action continued at a frantic pace and after 39 minutes it looked to be 2-2 when Blankley's 20-yard shot left Snaith unsighted but he recovered well to dive full-length and grab the ball far across to his right side on the goalline. Home man of the match Guest then slammed a shot against the bar from close range before Thomas brought the action to a halt for the interval.

Penistone dominated the second half and could easily have scored double the number of goals they eventually did. On the hour-mark, a game of head tennis across the Wakefield six-yard box proved entertaining but no one was able to get a crucial touch for hosts. It was 3-1 after 62 minutes when Guest's shot from the edge of the area bounced up just in front of goalkeeper Ruch and high into the roof of the net. A cross was then drilled across the area and found hirsute substitute Callum Lee at the far post in front of an open goal but he scooped the ball high over the bar. Ryan rose highest to power home a header from a free-kick to make it 4-1 after 67 minutes and the one-way traffic continued as the youngsters of Wakefield were brushed aside by the more physical home side. The goal of the game came after 75 minutes from Guest when he controlled a high through ball and blazed it into the net, all in one movement.

Coduri then cut in from the wing and his shot looked destined for the top corner until substitute goalkeeper Max Child stuck out a hand to divert it over the angle of bar and post for a corner. With six minutes to go, a cross was whipped in and found Coduri unmarked at the far post but he wasn't quick enough to react and fired his header over the bar from eight yards out. That proved to be the last action of the night, with a crowd of 237 warmed on a chilly evening by an entertaining encounter and some delicious sausage rolls from a thriving snack bar.

The result was a double disappointment for Wakefield who had discovered a day earlier that their hopes of elevation to the Northern Counties East League (NCE) had been dashed. The league had been operating with several vacancies and Wakefield were hopeful they would be considered for promotion from the Sheffield County League.

However, the FA has instead brought in clubs from the East Midlands to fill the gaps and chairman Mike Hegarty, speaking before the game, alongside chief executive Chris Turner, the former Manchester United, Sheffield Wednesday and Sunderland goalkeeper, said: "We were confident our application would be successful, especially with all the facilities we have at Featherstone and the plans we have drawn up. It is disappointing as the NCE will still be running a club short and they've shipped in teams from the East Midlands to make up the numbers."

No team has been promoted to the NCE from its Yorkshire feeder leagues. Ilkley did move up from the West Yorkshire League, but they have been placed in the North West Counties League, with Campion being moved sideways to join Steeton and Golcar on the other side of the Pennines. In their place, the FA have switched Clipstone, Ollerton, Rainworth MW, Shirebrook Town and Teversal from the East Midlands Counties League.

It was also disappointing for Penistone, who had been keeping their fingers crossed they would be given the nod for a place in the revamped Northern Premier League. A new division has been created and Penistone were first reserves for a call up.

Secretary Dave Hampshire explained. "We've just missed out twice on promotion to the NPL. We finished in the top three when only one team went up and have missed out this time because Covid interrupted after we'd been on a good run.

"We'd been doing well in the FA Vase and had lots of games in hand against teams lower down the league to boost our point-per-game score but didn't get the chance to play them."

Penistone had been ranked fifth in the points-per-game table, with three teams guaranteed to go up. There were doubts over whether they would all accept the invitation and fourth-placed Staveley had already pulled out, leaving Penistone in a hopeful position. Alas it was not to be, with Bridlington Town, Liversedge and Yorkshire Amateur named as new members of the NPL.

Penistone were given the Memorial Ground in 1949 by the Hinchliffe farming family, with a covenant that it could only be used for sporting use. It was in memory of those who had lost their lives in the First and Second World Wars. The present stand was built around the same time.

Hampshire made his Penistone 'debut' 59 years ago, as a five-year-old mascot. "I've been here man and boy ever since – as player, manager, and secretary for the last 30 years," he said.

The club's record crowd was 1,000-plus for a charity match with the Emmerdale All Stars but the largest 'official' attendance was 511 for a game against Pontefract Collieries as part of a Groundhoppers Weekend. "It was the Saturday night game and it was absolutely heaving. We lost 7-0. The spectators all came on buses and were queueing through the gates for food. Our homemade chilli con carne was amazing and got some good reviews.

"When I took over as secretary at the start of the 1990s, we were in an awful lot of debt and me and Terry Liles had to put money in to keep us going. We went round all the local business the club owed money to and offered to pay them back a bit at a time. If they hadn't accepted, they'd have got nothing because the club would have gone under. Thankfully they all agreed and it is that community spirit that has been at the heart of he club ever since. I was secretary and Terry was treasurer and we paid everything we owed over time. When Terry stepped aside, I got Jim Hinchcliffe to come in and together we carried on. In 1998 we put in for Lottery and Football Stadia grants to get an astroturf installed and that brought in much needed income and we've been building on that ever since. We had a bit of a lean patch when the clubhouse wasn't being used as much as it had been. We got more and younger people in to join the committee and that brought lots of new fresh ideas to get things moving forward again."

In 2002 the club had floodlights installed and that meant they could get bigger crowds for night games. "We didn't charge entry in the County League but the raffle and clubhouse sales meant our income went up," said Hampshire. "Harvey Ownsworth put us in a very good position as manager and when he left, the foundations had been laid for Ian Richard to take over with his brother Duncan as assistant.

"We set a target of winning the County Senior League, as we had never done that before, to get promotion to the NCE. We'd won the cup twice and reached a few finals but had never won the title. We finished fourth that season and, with the top five eligible for promotion, applied and were accepted – so we've still never won the County League!"

"From then on we've continued to build and with a higher level of football, bigger crowds have come, enabling us to keep progressing. From crowds of 80 to 120, suddenly we're getting more than 300 and they are growing."

A key figure behind the promotion of the club is Hackett, who is proud to fly the flag for grassroots football. "We keep the investment rolling in through lots of community involvement and by being such a friendly, welcoming club," he said. "We've now got 22 teams, including girls and women. As well as the first-team pitch, we've got another smaller one behind the far goal and more over the fence, as well as the Astroturf."

One of the players who progressed from Penistone's youth set-up is John Stones. The Manchester City centre back started his career as a five-year-old at Penistone, eventually moving into the Barnsley youth scheme, making his first-team debut at 17, before moving on to Everton. He appeared for England at u19, u20 and u21 levels, going on play more than 50 times for the full national side.

Of his time at Penistone, Stones recalled: "They got quite tasty at times and I remember playing up a few age groups, which I think helped me out, playing with the older lads. I got scouted for Barnsley's academy while I was still playing Sunday league football and I never played for any other local club after that."

Hackett is not from Penistone, but further afield from Sheffield. Nonetheless, he regards himself as a long-time local and is grateful for the boost he received from the club in his early days as a referee.

"One Saturday I was appointed to officiate at Penistone. I had no car in those days so caught the train but there was only one a day so I got her about 10.30am and had a walk up to the ground. A guy wearing a long leather coat was working on the pitch and asked what I was doing there. When I said I'd come to referee he said I was far too early but gave me a cup of tea and then said he was the chairman and asked if I'd mind refereeing an earlier game as the scheduled official had called off.

"I was 17 or 18 at the time and had been refereeing for about two years, it would have been 1962-ish. He wrote a really nice letter to the county FA and that helped me up the ladder."

Now Hackett's grandsons play for Penistone, as well as a granddaughter. "I used to come watch them on a Sunday morning and was asked my advice on how they could move from the County Senior League into the Northern Counties East League. I had lots of contacts and put them in touch with Dave Merrell at the NCE, who sent some people down to have look at the ground and advise them on what needed doing.

"It's a really well run, typical country club and the many volunteers they have are brilliant. The manager is vice-principal at the local school and most of the sponsors are local business people who come down to watch. We're also well supported by Penistone FM and on a Saturday Steve Wilson invites one of us to go on the radio for a chat about the club.

"People come to the clubhouse for a drink and a bite to eat and one suggested we run a 1906 Club. We get 100 people to pay £100 each to support the club and within two days of launching it, we were full. It's a really friendly, welcoming club and we have supporters who have sat in the same seats in the stand for years. That's what it's all about for me."

Hackett has been all around the world as a referee and was boss of the Premier League Referees Association but said football at that level seemed to have lost touch with the most important part of the game – the fans.

"I retired as a referee in 1995/6 but finished in the Premier League coming up to 50. I felt the training that was needed was getting too much. I did carry on locally until one day one of my colleagues asked what I was doing reffing at a local finals day. He said I was taking the place of young-up-and coming refs. I could see his point and didn't want to block their progress so I stopped. I keep busy now writing books and I always say it as I see it, so enjoy being on Twitter as well."

It is all a far cry from the earliest days of football in Penistone, when the club could have laid claim to the claim as the world's oldest club. That honour lies instead with Sheffield FC but three of the key people in their formation – John Shaw, John Marsh and John Ness Dransfield – all attended Penistone Grammar School.

What might have been…

As it was, Penistone Church FC were formed in 1906 from Penistone Choirboys and Penistone Juniors, who amalgamated. They played on grounds west of the Spread Eagle pub, roughly where the showground pitches are today.

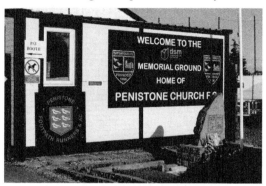

Above - Welcoming site: The Memorial Ground entrance at Penistone.

Right - Star guest? Gareth Bale is an unwitting addition to the clubhouse collage.

Below - Roll up! Penistone Church's club shop.

26. TAKING THE WATERS IS RECIPE FOR SUCCESS

Saturday, May 22, 2021
Campsmount School, Campsall
Askern Miners 3 Epworth Town Colts Blues 0
Doncaster Rovers Saturday League, Premier Division

Think Yorkshire spa towns and Harrogate, Scarborough and Bridlington will probably be the obvious choices. Askern is unlikely to feature. Although more noted now as a former mining town, the town centre lake offers a clue as to its previous heritage as a must-visit place for visitors from across the north.

Askern was just a small farming village when a Dr Short, in his book Mineral Waters of Yorkshire, referred to the local waters as having an unpleasant odour and taste. Over the next few decades, those waters started to gain a reputation as having healing powers. The Manor Baths were built and by the late 1800s the town had five bathhouses, with excursion trains laid on from as far afield as Liverpool to sample the waters.

Hotels and guesthouses were built to accommodate the influx of visitors and the spa town's waters were hailed as being rejuvenating with healing properties rated among the highest in the country. That all changed at the start of the 20th Century when a good seam of coal was discovered nearby. That led to the building of a mine in 1911 with hundreds of new residents moving to a purpose-built estate. This new population was at odds with the well-to-do visitors and, the death knell was sounded for the spa as visitors declined to a trickle.

Coal brought new prosperity to the town but the fumes and smoke created saw visitors steer clear. The closure of the pit in the 1990s saw the town struggle to survive but the influx of regeneration funds is bringing a recovery. The restorative waters continue to leak unheralded down a hillside and into the town's lake and it would appear the town's football club has been partaking of them in recent years.

While the spa brought visitors to the town, the flow of traffic has reversed in recent years with the keenest followers of Askern having had a fair old tour of the North and Midlands over the past 10 seasons. Stints in the Northern Counties East, Central Midlands and Doncaster Saturday Leagues have seen them rack up matches against 63 different opponents. These have included both the first and reserve teams of Rossington Main and as far afield as Easington on the East Yorkshire coast, Albion Sports and Eccleshill in Bradford, Cleethorpes and Grimsby Borough on the Lincolnshire coast, Knaresborough in North Yorkshire and south to Newark, as well as FA competition adventures against teams from Lancashire and Durham.

Now they've had to get used to a temporary new home as they continue a five-year plan to revisit many of those teams on their way back up the non-League ladder. End-of-season pitch renovation work at their Welfare Ground means their closing fixtures have been switched to their academy venue at Campsmount Academy in the neighbouring village of Campsall. It meant a second link of the season to Robin Hood for me – with a visit to the place where the legendary figure was reportedly married to Maid Marion.

Despite the unfamiliar and basic surroundings, it did not knock Askern off their stride as they marched towards the Doncaster Rovers Saturday League title. A 10th consecutive victory the following Saturday saw Askern crowned as champions.

Committee member Bracken Hart revealed how the Miners were determined to regain the level reached by their predecessors – Askern Welfare, Askern FC and Askern Villa, the same club under a variety of names. As Villa, they just missed out on promotion to the Premier Division of the NCE in 2009, but since then they have slipped down through the CML to the Donny League. The latest rebranding came last year when Askern Juniors merged with Askern FC to form Askern Miners. That has seen a change of colours with the home kit seeing the juniors' colours of red and blue stripes and the away one of black and white, representing the old Askern club.

"Askern FC were struggling for players and Sutton Rovers were playing at the ground so things were looking bleak, said

Hart. "However, we at Askern Juniors were thriving and made an approach to merge with the club. That happened but the new committee was all from the juniors, bar one member who stayed on from the other club – long-serving Jim Szmidt. All 300-plus of our players now play under the same banner and we have teams at all ages; from the three-to-five year old Mini Miners to two senior teams and an over-35 side. We're working on starting girls' teams and plan to have a second academy team next season."

Although off the field much has changed, with a 12-strong committee having a majority of female members, on it the team has a familiar look to it. "We have about six or seven players who have stayed on from the previous team but 95 per cent of our players are now from Askern and surrounding villages," said Hart. "Every one in today's team is an Askern lad and the average age is about 23.

"Previous managers brought in players from away and that didn't go down too well, when we have a population of about 14,000 to call on. We are lucky in that we've got a big local population to get players from and do not have any close neighbours. We're separate from Doncaster so our main rivals are probably Bentley and Thorne, now that Sutton Rangers have moved to Hatfield."

Focussing on youth and local seems to be working for the fans too with the revamped club pulling in 2-300 on a regular basis, although today's temporary venue saw only about a tenth of that in attendance.

"Askern were going really well in the NCE and our five-year-plan is to build gradually back to that level," said Hart. "If we win the league this season, we'll be ahead of that already. We want to progress back to the NCE via the CML. The Welfare Ground already meets NCE standards and the only problem we had was that the floodlights weren't bright enough. We've had new bulbs put in on the original stanchions so we're sorted now.

"We're also making a lot of effort to improve the pitch. It had been badly compacted so we've had work done on that and had the drains sorted and done verti-draining on it, with new top soil."

Plans are also being made to build a new clubhouse, while the current Welfare Club, which contains a bar and the changing rooms, has been refurbished. Two North Yorkshire rivals are also being reunited, with dug-outs from York City's Bootham Crescent, joining seats already in place from the former Athletic Ground home of Scarborough, said Hart, adding: "The floodlight stanchions also came from an old ground, but I'm not sure, which one. We are making good use of what we can get!"

At the Welfare Ground the club produces programmes and has a tea bar, to help raise funds, along with a raffle.

"Going forward, we're designing a new website and will also have new merchandise on sale," said Hart.

This is the latest twist in the club's long and eventful history. Established as Askern Welfare in 1924, they played in local Doncaster leagues for several decades. Their most famous player was Morgan Hunt. He started his career at Askern and went on to make 50 appearances for Doncaster Rovers between 1953-58, before short spells with Norwich City, Port Vale and Boston United. He returned to Askern as player-manager and later managed the Doncaster Belles Ladies team in 1979/80. He died aged 80 in 2012.

In 1967 Welfare won the Doncaster Senior League title for the only time and in 1992 were promoted to the Central Midlands Football League, progressing to the Northern Counties East League, with a change of name to Askern Villa. They made their FA Vase debut in 2010 and made a single appearance in the FA Cup a year later, losing to Thackley in the extra preliminary round.

In 2013 the club finished bottom of the league, conceding a record 173 goals. They were relegated back to the Central Midlands League and changed their name again, this time to Askern. In 2020, the club was renamed as Askern Miners and re-joined the Doncaster Saturday League, which is where I now find them.

Today's opponents are the reserve side of Lincolnshire League leaders Epworth Town Colts and are close to the bottom of the Doncaster League table, albeit with games in hand.

Askern made their title intentions clear from the start of a game they dominated, without ever pulling far enough ahead to relax. After seven minutes, Bailey May-Avil's free-kick saw Jacob Toomer rise highest to send a header narrowly wide. The first goal came a minute later when Chris Hancock ran down the left wing, doing well to keep a high bouncing ball under control, before stepping inside and unleashing a shot past Epworth goalkeeper Dan Bates.

Epworth came close to an unexpected equaliser after 23 minutes when they broke clear. The ball sat up nicely on the edge of the area for George Algar to crack it goalwards but Richard Groom was equal to the effort, punching the shot over the bar. A minute later it was 2-0 when Epworth defender Dan Debnam was caught on the ball and left trailing as Irwin ran through, rounded Bates and fired home. Several more chances came and went for the home side as they dominated proceedings but the interval arrived with only two goals in it.

The second half was virtually one-way traffic but Askern could only convert one more opportunity. Within seconds of the restart, an Askern effort from a corner was cleared off the goalline and the follow-up tipped over the bar by Bates. After 56 minutes, Alex Irwin's tricky run into the area saw him pull the ball back for Nathan Redmile but he cannoned his shot against the frame of the goal from eight yards out. A free-kick just after the hour mark saw a flick on provide Toomer with the third goal, nipping in to fire past Bates.

The final chance of the game fell to Epworth. However, hopes of an 83rd-minute consolation were dashed when a goal kick was headed on from the halfway line for Debnam to find space round the back of the home defence but he blazed over.

Up and at 'em: Askern's second home.

Playing it for laughs: The referee raises a smile.

27. BRENNAN'S STRIKE PROVES A WORTHY WINNER

Thursday, May 27, 2021
Skye Direct Stadium, Longfield Avenue, Golcar
Berry Brow 2 Newsome 1
Huddersfield League Barlow Cup, final

Berry Brow became the 41st different club to have their name inscribed on the Barlow Cup, in front of about 500 spectators at Golcar United's ground. The cup was first played for in 1936 and Brow became the deserved 85th winners of the trophy after beating the 2011 winners. Brow dominated the game and should have had the ribbons firmly flying from the cup's handles long before they had to hang on for victory after Newsome pulled a goal back in stoppage time.

The Huddersfield League was formed in 1898 and still runs eight divisions, only one less than at its peak capacity. Covid left the 2019/20 season unfinished and threatened to do the same to the current campaign after just eight weeks of action. However, the league committee acted quickly when it became obvious that grassroots football would be allowed to resume and ran a series of 'Champions League' groups to offer competitive action for the last couple of months of the normal season.

Rather than introduce new competition titles, the previous knockout tournaments were run as mini-leagues with teams from the top two divisions competing in the Barlow Cup. The four group winners met at the semi-final stage and it was Berry Brow and Newsome who emerged victorious for the chance to play off for the trophy at Golcar. The football-starved fans turned out in numbers to see the encounter and the bar and refreshment kiosk at the North West Counties League club was doing a roaring trade.

League president Margaret Whitaker was manning the entrance gate, taking the £3 entry fee, with other committee members busy running the raffle. Secretary Howard Young was sitting looking after the trophy and medals in the middle of the impressive stand, which bears the names of all the supporters who raised the funds to enable Golcar to take their place at football's level 10.

Young explained that this was the first time the final had been held at Golcar. Traditionally it was held at Huddersfield Town but he said: "We played it at Town's ground until they went into the Premiership, first at Leeds Road then at the new stadium.

"There wasn't a final last year due to Covid but the year before it was held at Emley. It has been great to see the progress being made by Huddersfield League clubs to reach higher levels – Emley, Golcar, Shelley and Marsden have all done really well."

The last time I visited Golcar was eight years ago and it was just a pitch with a barrier round it. Crampons would have been handy for the visiting Steeton players, who discovered how steeply sloped the pitch ran from touchline to touchline. The transformation has been incredible. As well as now offering a level playing field, the newly-named Skye Direct Arena also has the smart seated stand on the halfway line, a block of covered terracing next to the clubhouse and bar and a low covered enclosure behind the near goal and the other side of the changing rooms and food kiosk. Floodlights complete the upwardly mobile metamorphosis. With the nearside of the pitch now several feet lower than previously, it allows excellent sight-lines for fans gathered along the standing area, giving a panoramic view over the tops of the dug outs to the tree-lined far touchline. All but a small section behind the far goal has hard standing and work is ongoing to complete that.

"They've done a lot of work here," said Young. "The pitch used to have a real slope on it and when they levelled it, the pile of earth they took off hid the houses behind the goal from sight."

Tonight's crowd validated the league's decision to run competitive end-of-season games but Young said that, even so, he had been amazed at how well the public had responded. "The semi-final between Berry Brow and Linthwaite was sure to get a big crowd because they are local rivals but I was surprised quite how many turned up. There was more than 300 for the Richardson Cup final the other night at Shelley."

The 2017 Division Two champions made a solid start to their aim of capturing the cup for the first time and forced a string of corners in the opening minutes as Newsome struggled to keep them at bay. Fans were left baffled by which team was which in the early stages. They both sported their usual colours but the red and black stripes of Newsome were hard to distinguish from their opponents' maroon and blue stripes. With both teams also wearing dark coloured shorts and socks, it made decision making tougher for referee Mick Denton and his assistants Gareth Thomas and Michael Coles.

Brow came close to an early goal when Joe Brennan powered a header narrowly wide from a corner. The first Newsome attack came after seven minutes with a speculative shot from the edge of the penalty area flying over. After 11 minutes, a deep cross reached Brow's Tom Oakes at the far post and his effort drew a superb point-blank save from goalkeeper George Kitchen. The respite was brief as Brow took the lead three minutes later when a shot was blocked and the ball fell for Oakes to slam it high into the net.

Another flurry of comers created pandemonium in the Newsome area with frantic blocks and goalkeeper and defenders throwing their bodies in the way to keep their goal safe but Brow were unable to find a way past. A rare excursion into the Brow half saw Newsome go close to an unexpected equaliser when Kyle Walton's tricky, twisty run into the penalty area ended with him curling a shot just wide of the far post. More pressure from Brow brought them a second goal on the stroke of half-time. They were awarded a free-kick near the touchline, 30 yards out. With attackers and defenders lined up ready to rush in at the far post, Brennan curled the ball straight in at the near post for the goal that later earned him the man of the match award. That did seem a little odd as Newsome goalkeeper Kitchen really did repel everything but the sink for much of the game and was felt by many people to be a more worthy recipient.

Two minutes after the break, Brennan came close again when his overhead kick saw goalkeeper Kitchen get down quickly to push the ball round a post. Newsome thought they had gained a foothold in the match after 56 minutes when it was 'shots in' as a barrage of efforts were kept out until the ball fell for Dean Siddiq to slam home but the flag was already up for offside. Mark McSherry's cross-cum-shot from the touchline left the Brow goalkeeper grasping thin air but the ball dropped just on the outside of the far post to roars and gasps from the stand behind the attacker As Brow eased off the pressure, with the game seemingly won, Newsome piled forward and were rewarded in the fourth minute of stoppage time when they gained a free-kick, just outside the penalty area. Walton's effort took a deflection and found its way into the back of the net in a scramble. Brow immediately shut up shop and offered no chance of an equaliser in the remaining two minutes.

It was just left for the dejected Newsome players and the match officials to receive their awards before Berry Brow celebrated their trophy win in traditional style with a bottle of Champagne showering the grandstand seats.

Numbers game: The teams line up for the Barlow Cup final.

Lofty ambitions: Taking in the view at Golcar.

Champions! Berry Brow celebrate their win.

28. LOST IN A LAND OF GIANTS

Saturday, May 29, 2021
Yorkshire Payments Stadium, St Giles Road, Hove Edge,
Brighouse
Liversedge 4 Penistone Church 0
Yorkshire Trophy final

Goals in the opening minutes of both halves sent Liversedge on the way to a comfortable victory in the inaugural Yorkshire Trophy final. The newly-promoted Northern Premier League side proved to have far too much fire power for Penistone to handle and a solid rearguard ensured there was never a likelihood of David slaying this particular set of Goliaths.

However, the real victors in this hastily arranged tournament was football in general, according to Brighouse media manager Damo Wales. "100 per cent it's been a success," he said. "No matter who the winners were, football has been the main winner. We've got football back on the pitch, crowds back in the ground and given football back to our communities. We're already planning next year's event, which will be bigger and better. We hope to make it an annual tournament, probably pre-season. We expect those teams that had to pull out will want to be involved and, hopefully, there'll be more wanting to join us."

The tournament was originally planned to take part in April and 12 teams were to be involved. Unfortunately, a change in the rules for the relaxation of the coronavirus lockdown meant the return of fans to grounds was delayed. "The idea for the tournament came from our manager Vill Powell," said Wales. "All clubs had their season curtailed and he wanted to get some competitive friendlies back. When the news came that we couldn't have fans until May 17, we lost eight of the clubs. They said they needed the summer to do work on their pitch and didn't want to risk damaging it."

With Campion, Garforth Town, Eccleshill United, Emley, Ossett United, Steeton, Silsden, and Thackley all pulling out, it left just

Golcar, Liversedge and Penistone, alongside host club Brighouse. It also brought a change of competition title after an online poll had voted for it to be called the Covid Cup, narrowly beating the Yorkshire Isolation Trophy. However, Brighouse decided that references to the coronavirus pandemic were inappropriate, in light of the massive loss of life across the globe. In a statement, the club said: "We felt the poll to determine the tournament name was not thought through properly and the implications of the suggested names were ill-considered and insensitive to the ongoing situation. Therefore the tournament will now be known as The Yorkshire Trophy. We apologise for any offence this may have caused, it was not our intention as a community football club."

"We were panicking because we thought we'd have to call it all off and would be left with no football until we started back in July," said Wales. "Then Nostell and Wakefield said they wanted to get involved and we were up to six clubs. It meant it was viable and so Vill and I sat down to work out how we'd play things. With only one group it meant we had problems with some clubs being unavailable on certain days of the week, so, instead, we decided on two groups of three.

"It's gone really well and we've had about five crowds of more than 400 with a high of almost 700. For a friendly competition that's incredible and the clubs have been delighted with the responses from the fans."

The qualifying groups saw Brighouse win both their ties; 1-0 against Penistone and 2-0 at Wakefield, with Penistone finishing runners-up after a 5-1 win over Sheffield & Hallamshire County League side Wakefield. The other group was topped by Golcar United after a 5-2 win against Nostell and a 2-2 draw with Liversedge. 'Sedge beat Nostell 2-1 to secure second place.

The semi-finals paired Brighouse with Liversedge and Golcar with Penistone and both encounters went 3-0 in favour of the away team. A third-place play-off took place at Brighouse earlier in the day with the hosts going down 4-3 on penalties to Golcar after a thrilling 3-3 draw. The North West Counties Leaguers took a 2-0 lead only for Brighouse to pull back to go 3-2 up before conceding a late equaliser.

And so to the final with a crowd of 364 consisting mainly of neutrals. As well as a fair smattering of Brighouse fans, staying on from their earlier match and ahead of the screening of the Champions League final in the clubhouse later in the day, the proliferation of Scouse and Geordie accents and conversations based around the best local real ale pubs, a large number of groundhoppers were also adding a 'tick' to their tallies. There are some real gems of 'boozers' apparently, highlighted by the number of advertising hoardings advertising local hostelries.

As soon as the teams lined up, it was obvious Penistone had a giant task on their hands. The Liversedge line-up included several daunting figures with John Cyrus, Jack Steers, Oliver Fearon, Gavin Allott and early substitute Charlie Marshall all looking like they'd overdone the Weetabix as children. That aerial presence soon made an impact and after only two minutes Fearon crossed from the right wing for Allott to draw a great save out of Church goalkeeper Adam Rhodes with a close range header. That was only a brief let-off though because three minutes later the Blues went ahead when right-back Adam Porritt crossed to the far post and man mountain captain Cyrus powered home a header. Liversedge squandered a great chance to double their advantage after 18 minutes when they played tip-tap football in the six-yard box and twice passed the ball across the face of goal when it looked easier to score with no-one on hand to knock the ball the six inches needed into the yawning net.

They continued to dominate the game, pressing hard, but Penistone stood firm and always looked dangerous on the break, slicing through the Liversedge midfield with ease, only to founder on the rocks of their opponents' twin centre backs Cyrus and Steers. The pair swatted aside any threat of a Penistone revival, winning everything in the air and on the ground, with a deceptive turn of pace obliterating most opportunities for their Northern Counties East League opponents to get back into the game.

The nearest Church came to an equaliser came just before the interval. First a Liversedge goal kick was headed back towards goal from the halfway line and John Pugh ran clear but goalkeeper Jordan Porter was out quickly to block at the expense of a corner. Two minutes later wideman Eddie Newsome crossed for Nick

Guest and his header looked destined for the top corner of the Liversedge net until Porter soared to his left to tip the ball away and was then quickly back on his feet to block the follow-up shot for an incredible double save.

That double warning earned an on-field team talk from the Liversedge management team at the interval, while their opponents took to the shelter of the changing rooms. As the alcohol from the busy clubhouse started to loosen tongues, more chants came from the terraces in support of Liversedge. But generally the atmosphere was very un-cup final like, more like a pre-season friendly, perhaps due to the fact the host club was not involved.

The game was over as a contest within a minute of the second half getting under way when a Penistone attack broke down. The ball was shipped out quickly to the Liversedge left winger and he raced away before crossing for Allott to tap in one of the easiest chances of his long non-League career. After that, Liversedge simply went through the motions, clamping down on any Penistone ingressions into their half, doing just enough to keep them pinned back. It was 3-0 after 72 minutes when a free-kick to the far post saw the ball knocked back for Fearon to control it on his chest and fire over his head high into the net. The final goal came in the last minute and was unfortunate for Penistone. Fearon broke clear but his effort was blocked by the goalkeeper, only for the ball to bounce up wickedly and ricochet off chasing defender Luke McGinnell into the net via the underside of the crossbar.

Penistone manager Ian Richards, speaking to his club's social media channel, felt the scoreline did not do justice to his team's efforts. "It's disappointing to lose any final but I didn't think it was a 4-0 performance," he said. "I thought we did well, particularly in the first half, playing a team of physical, tall, aggressive players, who played to those strengths.

"It took a public dressing down on the pitch from their manager to lift Liversedge. The goal just after half-time really killed us but the players stuck at it, considering we had nine regulars missing and two playing with injuries. I don't like to make excuses but they all gave it 100 per cent. I can't fault the boys to a man. We were unfortunate to concede four but the goals could have been prevented. We just lost our way a bit but kept going to the end. There were some outstanding performances and we will be in a strong position to win the NCE Premier and do well in the FA Vase next season. It's been nice to play in a competitive tournament in what has been a really unique and challenging season for a number of reasons. Our thanks go to Brighouse Town and Vill Powell for organising it."

Among the crowd for the final was a fair number of families and youngsters, and that is one set of fans the host club are keen to continue to attract. Media manager Wales said attracting the younger generation of fans to the club was his main aim.

"In the past, the only people who knew there was a game on were readers of the Brighouse Echo," he said. With newspaper readership generally declining, Wales was keen to spread the word further and try to attract younger fans.

He now manages a team of six volunteers to ensure the club receives maximum publicity across a wide range of media, still including the local newspaper. "We have our own radio station and a presence on Instagram, Twitter, Facebook and Tik Tok," he said. "We have match reporters and photographers, all keen to spread the word."

Wales own role entails updating the club website and social media management. "There are graphics and videos to arrange, with highlights packages and goal gifs as well as the more traditional matchday team sheets to print and distribute," he said. "I've also been helping get sponsors for player and managers and am currently involved in a season ticket campaign and setting up an online retail club shop."

All these innovations are aimed at broadening the club's appeal to the local population and increasing crowds do seem to show that Wales and his team are making a success of things, helped no doubt by the club's onfield success.

Left - Junior star: The Liversedge goalkeeper is put through his paces.
Below - We've won the cup! Jubilant Liversedge players.
Bottom - Pay and display: Queuing up to get into the Yorkshire Payments Stadium.

29. THORNTON'S DOUBLE CREATES CUP HISTORY

Monday, May 31, 2021
Hampden Road, Mexborough
Joker 1 Swinton Athletic 2
Montagu Charity Cup final

Two goals in two minutes on the hour mark from Matt Thornton gave Swinton victory in the historic Mont and earned them a place in the record books.

And what a history book the Mexborough Montagu Hospital Charity Cup, to give it its full name, makes. First played for in 1897 when it was won by Ecclesfield, 2022 will see its 125th anniversary, with the final still being played at its original home, 122 editions of the competition along. It was competed for throughout the Second World War and in all but two years of the First World War, with 1900 the only other blank year.

More than 60 teams have their names inscribed on the magnificent trophy, including Doncaster Rovers, a variety of Mexborough clubs, Swinton Discharged Soldiers & Sailors, Jump Home Guard and Yorkshire Tar Distillers, plus an array of pub, works, social club, village and semi-professional sides.

The tale of the Mont is told in glorious detail by Chris Brook on the www.montagucup.com website and within its pages are tales of derring do, World Cup players, FA Cup winners, a player who scored in the Football League in the afternoon and in the cup in the evening. It is the earlier years that have created the most interest for Brook. "A mate of mine told me that a player who had scored in a Totty Cup final and also scored in the Mont and had gone on to score in the FA Cup final and at the World Cup finals, including playing against England," said Brook. "I didn't really believe him but discovered it was true."

The Mont's little brother, the Totty Cup (a competition covering a similar geographical area for primary schools) was won by Brampton Ellis School in 1939 and 1940, kicking off an incredible story for a young lad from West Melton – George Robledo. Robledo scored four goals in both those finals and went on to score the winner for Wath Wanderers in the 1944 Mont final. Within seven years the young Chilean immigrant was making a name for himself on a far bigger stage – playing at Wembley for Newcastle United in the 1951 and 1952 FA Cup finals, scoring the winner in the latter and becoming the first non-British player to be Football League top scorer. Robledo played for his native Chile in the 1950 World Cup finals, including a game against England, where his broad Yorkshire accent proved confusing!

The Yorkshire Chilean was such a legend in the game that John Lennon drew a childhood picture of his FA Cup final goal against Arsenal. The former Beatle later used it as the cover artwork on his fifth solo album, the 1974 record Walls & Bridges. Robledo returned to Chile and died in 1989 but his daughter, Elizabeth, was due to visit South Yorkshire in 2020 to unveil a blue plaque on her father and uncle's childhood home in West Melton. Covid meant that did not happen but she has been invited back in 2022.

Robledo, as well as his brother Ted, who also moved from Barnsley to Newcastle before eventually losing his life at sea in mysterious circumstances, were not the only players to progress from the Mont to greater things. Leeds United and England World Cup-winning trainer Les Cocker scored a hat-trick in the 1942 final for Manvers Main, while many others enjoyed successful Football League careers after their appearance in the Mont, including Lionel Smith, who earned six full England caps while playing for Arsenal and Watford, and Joe Beresford, an FA Cup winner with Preston North End.

Another cup tale tells of Wally Ardron, who scored in the Football League in the afternoon for Rotherham United and in the Mont final in the evening, having started his day at 2am, working a shift on the railway. To add to his heroism, he rode a bicycle between each of the day's engagements!

The Bennett family, from Mexborough, were probably the region's most successful sporting family and all boasted a Mont pedigree. William Bennett and four of his sons were also in the Mexborough team that beat Barnsley in the FA Cup. Of those sons, Walter won two FA Cups with Sheffield United, Mickey won the FA Cup with Sheffield Wednesday and George and Tip both played for Barnsley. Grandson Walter also played for Barnsley, while another grandson, William Haigh, was a world champion boxer.

Joannah Bennett also hit the headlines as football hooligan. She was a huge woman who would stand no rough play when her husband and boys were involved. She would often go on the pitch to confront referees and opposing players alike, eventually receiving a ground ban order after trying to punch a player during a Mexborough v Barnsley St Peter's derby.

Former school teacher Brook's interest in the Mont came about by accident, after starting to research the history of the Totty Cup. "It has been going almost as long as the Mont and I did some research to try to find pictures and reports of all the finals," he said. "While I was doing that, I took some screen shots of the Mont, as both finals were played around the same time of year. Barry Dalby, the Mont organiser, heard about it and asked if I'd do some research on the Mont, and that's where the website came from."

The website records in painstaking detail reports from most of the 120-plus finals with contemporary newspaper reports and pictures, plus the stories of many of the famous names associated with the cup over the year. "When I reached 1960 I thought I was nearly there but there's still 60 year to go and I've hit a bit of a wall so will need to go to libraries to see the microfiches," said Brook. "Unfortunately, the more recent ones are not online like the earlier days. It's probably the last 20 years that will be the most difficult as papers didn't cover the depths of sport they'd done previously."

The latest chapter belongs to Swinton Athletic though who, with victory today, became the club with the most wins to their name – moving one ahead of Wombwell Main and Mexborough Main Street – with a total of eight. They first won it in 1964 and again in 1968, 1972, 1980, 1986 and 1989 before enduring a 31-year wait for their seventh title last year.

All proceeds from the competition are give to the Mexborough

Montagu Hospital and over the last 72 years that has seen more than £70,000 handed over to the Comforts Fund – providing items not available through the NHS for the benefit of patients, staff and visitors to the town's Montagu Hospital in Adwick Road. The hospital was originally funded by donations from local industries, churches and various charitable organisations as well as wealthy local residents – topped up by revenue generated from the Montagu Cup.

Today's match pitted the Sheffield County Senior League Premier Division holders with the 2019 winners, Joker, from the Rotherham Sunday League.

It was an 11am kick-off but the club car park was already full an hour before that and the teams were out on the pitch, preparing for the big game. Signage around the ground and on the stand is in the name of Mexborough Athletic but no senior club of that name has played here for more than two decades. A variety of town clubs have used the ground though, from Mexborough FC way back in 1884 to Mexborough Town Athletic, who folded in 2001, and the ground has hosted Midland League, Yorkshire League and FA Cup matches during its 130-year-plus history. Swathes of concrete terracing around three sides of the historic ground means it is easy to picture how it used to hold crowds of 5,000-plus for this Easter spectacular. Covid meant this year's final had to be delayed in order to allow fans to attend and about 600 responded, all paying their £3 and making donations to boost the hospital funds.

After signing in and having a squirt of sanitiser, fans were allowed through the gate to collect their free programme and a copy of the local Around Town magazine, which included a feature on the cup. Hot food and refreshments, all donated by local firms, were being served from a pair of gazebos, with proceeds going to a local youngster with a cleft lip. The clubhouse was open later in the day with a free flow of beer ensuring a cheery disposition to the growing crowd.

The Montagu Cup is no Sunday morning kick around. It is deadly serious and players from both sides looked very professional in their preparation, until I spotted the Joker No.17 sneaking off behind the stand for a call of nature.

Swinton are now the tenants at Hampden Road and so enjoyed home advantage, although for most of the first hour of the game it was Joker who looked the more likely winners. They just about shaded a first half bereft of chances but were dealt a double blow just before the 60-minute mark. A tricky run from Swinton's left winger saw him deliver an inviting cross to the far post where Thornton was waiting to head it back across goalkeeper Jamie Bailey and into the net.

Two minutes later Thornton advanced on goal and lobbed Bailey from the edge of the area to double his tally. So it was Swinton who went forward to collect their historic eighth Mont, with No.8 Shaun Mitchell named as man of the match.

Joker did not go home empty-handed though. As well as individual mementoes, the team also received the rather impressive Bernard Hodgkinson Memorial Shield as runners-up.

Every town and many villages used to run charity cup competitions for a local hospital or organisation. Over the years most have fallen by the wayside but the Montagu Cup continues. Brook thinks the reason is that it has been adaptable over the years. "It got really big during the Second World War and the final would attract crowds of more than 5,000 with professional players taking part," he said. "When it started it was mainly teams involved with the local churches, then it was teams formed by soldiers before mining sides took over. Adaptability has been key and the decision was taken in the 1980s or 90s to allow Sunday sides to enter, alongside the usual Saturday teams that have always played in it.

"That does cause issues with players having to choose which of their weekend teams to represent. In this year's semi-final there was about half-a-dozen Swinton Athletic players who could have turned out for Dog Daisy (a Mexborough pub side), while the same could be said for their opponents."

Above − Phone a friend? Decision time in the Montagu Cup final.

Left − Winner: Matt Thornton is congratulated after opening the scoring.

Below − History makers: Joker lift the cup.

30. MEN AGAINST BOYS BUT CHARITY IS THE WINNER

Saturday, June 5, 2021, 10.30am
Keepmoat Stadium, Doncaster
Life for a Kid All Stars 1 Autism Athletic 6
Football for Autism 6

The goals flowed and cash poured in for charity at Doncaster's Keepmoat Stadium. It was the venue for the sixth football fundraising event for the Hull-based Life For A Kid charity and raised more than £6,000. The teams consisted of players who had raised a minimum of £200 for the charity and included former Featherstone Rovers and Hull FC rugby league star Richard Whiting.

A busy car park at the 15,000-plus capacity all-seater stadium augured well for the match attendance. However, it was not the only event on at the 15-year-old £32million complex. One of the neighbouring 3G pitches was hosting a Yorkshire Christian League match between Bentley and Armley, another area was the venue for the Young Drivers programme , while the stadium's West Stand had been commandeered for use as Covid vaccination centre. The complex is also home to a mini stadium, containing a six-lane running track and 500-seater stand alongside a pitch used by Doncaster Athletics Club, Doncaster Rugby League Academy and American football team, the Doncaster Mustangs. The stadium also has conference and banqueting facilities and multi-functional spaces, all a far cry from the Belle Vue ground that had been Rovers' home for 85 years.

The last time I was at Doncaster Rovers they were a non-League team playing in a dilapidated old stadium. How things have changed, they are now flying high in League One at a spick and span ground firmly at the heart of their community.

Every time I visited Belle Vue it seemed to have got a bit grimmer – a bit more graffiti here, paint missing there, a stand showing the effects of an arson attack everywhere...

However, Rovers have been keen not to bury all their history and the new ground pays tribute to supporters, players and officials who have gone before in their 142-year history. As well as montages of club legends, the stadium walls full are full of bricks and plaques devoted to fans and sponsors.

By 10am today, just 30 minutes before the scheduled kick-off, a short queue had built outside the turnstiles. Inside, a small section of the East Stand was open for the charity encounter, more than ample space for the 70-or-so supporters who had turned up to watch their friends, husbands, boyfriends, sons and fathers in action. What the match meant to many of the players was illustrated when I overheard one of them talking to his family over the pitch perimeter wall saying: "This is the only chance I'll ever get to play at a ground like this."

When the teams emerged, it appeared the white-shirted Autism Athletic would not stand a chance as their opponents were all referees. Kitted out in black shirts, their 12 men lined up for the kick-off until, closer inspection revealed that 11 of them did in fact have numbers on the back of their shirts – black ones! Thankfully, the players wore a collection of different coloured shorts and socks, to aid identification slightly, although this reporter did have to note other attributes to differentiate them. Confusion still reigned until a break for drinks on the stifling hot morning gave the referee chance to pull on a blue bib to differentiate who was in charge.

One of the Life For A Kid All Stars was in familiar garb though, with East Riding referee Jack Wilkin taking a break from officiating to sample life from the other end of the whistle.

Players ranged in age from 13 to 47 and in height from barely five foot to six-foot plus. The All Stars fielded the much younger-looking team but made a lively start, forcing several corners in the opening minutes. Many of the players were only just teenagers but were not out of place and young goalkeeper Danny Pullen was in terrific form, keeping out a string of what looked goalbound efforts, before having to be substituted in the second half with an injury.

The first chance of the game came after two minutes when

All Stars' Tom Giblin, recognised by his man bun/long hair – depending on the time in the game – had a header from a corner saved by Anthony Town. The blacks continued to push but were caught on the break after seven minutes when Whiting showed his professional skills, albeit with the wrong-shaped ball, to hammer in a glorious opening goal from fully 30 yards. To be fair, before his career with the oval ball took off, he was on Barnsley FC's books as a junior, so it was no surprise that he was the stand-out player in midfield, pulling the strings of all the Athletic attacks. Four minutes later a through ball released Freddie Laycock but his shot hit a post and the ricochet was cleared off the line by a covering All Stars defender. After 25 minutes, Wayne Audsley crossed for Riccardo Seaton at the far post but his attempt at a diving header saw him just fail to connect when he launched himself in spectacular style at the All Stars' goal.

Pullen and his defenders were in hectic action on the half-hour mark. A shot was blocked and the loose ball looked destined for the net when Laycock sent it towards the top corner but the goalkeeper reacted quickly to paw it away and two follow-up efforts were blocked in the six-yard box as defenders threw themselves bravely in the way to protect their goal. Pullen took centre stage again soon after when he tipped a howitzer from Dean Sharp over the bar. Six-foot-plus Sharp certainly stood out. The Athletic captain dwarfed the adult players next to him and he was a real giant in comparison to the young lads who tried in vain to outjump him, barely reaching his hips! With no ball boys at the stadium, it meant players had a busy time having to go up into the seats to retrieve the ball from wayward shots and hefty clearances.

Half-time arrived with Athletic leading by a single goal. They had chance to double that advantage early in the second half when the referee spotted an infringement in the All Stars' penalty area and pointed to the spot, despite no appeals from the Athletic players and a look of bafflement from both teams. However, Sharp stepped up and, in an act of charity as well as sportsmanship, simply tapped the ball to Pullen.

Ben Norris' shot from the edge of the area took a big deflection but Pullen adjusted quickly to save but he was beaten after 54 minutes when a shot was blocked but Sharp curled the loose ball into the top corner of the net. It was 3-0 after an hour and this time the penalty was converted after an attacker was tripped as he headed for goal. Norris stepped forward and blasted the spot kick past Pullen's despairing dive.

The All Stars registered a rare shot after 64 minutes when Jordan Kinsley (reporter's note: blue tape on socks and fluorescent boots) received the ball on the wing, cut inside and curled a shot that looked destined for the top corner until Town threw out an arm to tip the ball over the bar. Ian Garner then fired in a deflected effort on the Athletic goal but Town adjusted quickly to scramble across to make the save.

The fourth goal came after 67 minutes when Laycock created space for himself in the area and blasted the ball past Pullen from close range. That was Pullen's last action of the game as he had to go off with a dislocated shoulder and needed treatment at hospital. Garner again went close for the All Stars when he took the ball round Town but defenders got back quickly to block his shot on the line. The All Stars finally got a reward after 75 minutes when the ball was played into the penalty area and Giblin reacted quickly to send a stunning volley past Town and high into the net.

Substitute Ellis Yorke (note: young, blond, green stripe on socks) came on for the All Stars and played an impressive cameo role, running at defenders and giving the Athletic defence cause for concern. He was unlucky with one deflected effort, which Town again had to be alert for to react and save. Athletic weathered the storm and almost added a fifth when Audsley broke clear, drew the goalkeeper but sent his lob wide of the target from the edge of the penalty area.

However, two minutes later the white shirts notched up their nap-hand when the ball was played through for substitute Lewis Kelsey to hammer home. The final goal came in the third minute of stoppage time. A big boot forward saw Audsley gallop clear from his own half before dummying the substitute goalkeeper and leaving him on his backside as he tapped home. Two minutes later the whistle was blown on an entertaining encounter, warmly applauded by the crowd who appreciated the effort put in by both teams, who kept going to the end, despite the hot weather.

The main winners though were those children who will benefit from the Life For A Kid sensory room in Hull. Charity founder Dean Hoggard said: "A facility such as this has many benefits for children with special needs as it creates a stimulating and yet calming atmosphere. Among other things it can help to improve hand and eye co-ordination and develop language skills.

"The overactive child can be calmed and the inactive become interested. All young children can benefit from using a sensory room to develop fundamental sensory skills needed in later life. It will give them a chance to explore their feeling and to become interested in their environment. This calming environment is a place where parents/carers will have time to bond with their children, providing a restful and peaceful experience in today's busy and sometimes stressful lifestyles."

The centre, at 2 Leonard Street, Hull, HU3 1SA, is free of charge for children with Special Educational needs.

The charity football match is just one of the ways funds have been raised for the foundation. Previous matches have featured top stars including Manchester United FA Cup winners Lee Sharp and Lee Martin; Noel Whelan, of Leeds United; Liverpool pair David Speedie and Alan Kennedy; as well as former England international Emile Heskey. Kennedy is a big supporter of the foundation and was due to be a guest speaker at a sportsman's dinner in Hull in July.

It is not just football that help the foundation though, as Hoggard added: "We have two rugby league events at Featherstone Rovers in July and our main fundraising is via rugby league charity games and our charity team Rugby League All Stars."

The Keepmoat Stadium was an appropriate venue for the latest charity match because Doncaster Rovers are big supporters of special needs. In a season where the greed of football clubs hit the headlines following the failed European Super League, how refreshing it was to see a professional club pouring benefits back into the community.

They play their part in supporting people with autism on first-team match days as Nick Gillott, of the Club Doncaster Foundation explained: "The club mascot is Donny the Dog and he has a 'kennel' in the stand where we put on various events and activities for the youngsters before games. Once the match starts, that room is an autism safe room, somewhere where anyone feeling anxious in a big crowd can escape to for some peace and quiet."

Community development manager Gillott said Club Doncaster Foundation works alongside Doncaster Rovers FC, Doncaster Rovers Belles and Doncaster Rugby League to bring professional sport into the local community. "We work with a wide range of partners to provide sport and physical activity opportunities to anyone within the Doncaster community and surrounding areas. We are a non-profit, self-funding registered charity that has achieved more than 30 years of inspiring positive change, participation in sport, physical activity and education within the Doncaster Borough and internationally. We utilise the social reach of the professional sports clubs and community stadium to challenge lifelong habits, inspire positive change and motivate sustained participation in sport, physical activity, training and education.

"Working across four key areas, with a total of 35 projects, the team amassed an aggregate attendance of 209,475 across 2018/19."

Gillott said: "The Foundation is the charity arm of Doncaster Rovers and we are based at the stadium. We have a number of projects at 26 schools across the borough and we run breakfast clubs, after-school clubs and PE lessons. One of those projects is Kicks, which is funded by the Premier League and is all about supporting active lives in the most deprived areas of the community, aimed at reducing anti-social behaviour. We also support men's and women's health and have started a bike library. We charge people a £10 deposit and they have the use of a cycle for a week. It's to be used instead of a car to increase physical activity and we're also working with the Job Centre so people can get to interviews and appointments."

Last month the foundation opened a community gym at the stadium, which they claim is the cheapest in Doncaster with every penny that people pay to use it going back into the community.

"The football club is brilliant with us and supports everything we do," added Gillott. "They are very supportive. Every year we are given items of football kit from the first team – kit, training gear, football boots. Last year we were given 1,000 items to distribute around the community with nine schools among the beneficiaries."

Rovers are also one of only five clubs to be part of Football Welcomes, helping refugees and asylum seekers. Another scheme, Rovers Care, runs from October to December and last year saw more than 700 care packages delivered to socially isolated and 50-plus people in the borough. "Every member of the first team squad went out delivering," said Gillott. "The New York Times sent a reporter across to film it.

"We've also got a college in the stadium and have 122 students in full-time education up to degree level doing sports courses. We're funded by the NHS and CCG (clinical commissioning group) for an eight-week health intervention course mainly for the over-35s. It's a different subject each week over an eight-week course – the first part each week is learning about PE, mental health, dietary habits or something similar and the second half is a physical activity. Since we started it in 2017, 250 men have lost more than a ton in their aggregate weight.

"After eight weeks we don't just tick a box and send them on their way. We run Fit Rovers Vets from 7-9pm every Thursday. The social centre is open from 6pm and they can come early for a chat and too socialise. From 7 it's cycling or circuit training and from 8 football, cycling or badminton. It costs just £3 for all three hours. All the money goes back into the club and it's up to their own committee what they spend it on. So far they have financed a two-day Yorkshire Three Peaks walk for 16 of them and also took part in a Tough Mudder – endurance run. Men aged 35-plus are the hardest group to engage with but at one session we had 192 of them, some having started back in 2017."

In the club: The Keepmoat home of sport in Doncaster.

Paying homage: The teams thank their supporters

Looking good: A stand view of the Football for Autism encounter.

31. CITY AIM FOR THE BRIGHT LIGHTS

Saturday, June 5, 2.30pm
Mallorie Park, Ripon
Ripon City 1 Brighouse Sports 3
West Yorkshire League, Division Two

Of the seven Yorkshire cities, teams from four of them have enjoyed life at the very top of the English football pyramid – Leeds, Bradford, Sheffield and Hull.

A fifth, York, are languishing in the National League North but have played as high as the old Second Division, while Wakefield are making encouraging noises about plans to be in the Football League within 10 years. But what of the seventh? Little old Ripon have slightly lesser ambitions.

They may currently be at the 13th level, in Division Two of the West Yorkshire League, but after a few years in the doldrums, they are gearing up for progress. Unfortunately they face a significant handicap.

Ideally, they would love to move up towards the Northern Counties East League but to do so, they would need to leave their Mallorie Park ground that has been home for about a century.

"The simple fact is that to progress we would have to move from here," said club treasurer Gary Camplejohn. "We were refused planning permission to put a fence round the ground so we know it would be a waste of time to even apply for floodlights to go up."

But a move to somewhere suitable is no easy task. Although a city in the traditional West Riding, Ripon is far from the stereotypical 'Wessie' city. Now under North Yorkshire County Council, its magnificent cathedral gives it city status, even though it is no more than a market town in size, with a population of less than 17,000. That limits options for a new ground and the meandering routes of the city's two rivers, the Skell and the Laver, reduce available land further. Much of the historic centre is also protected, while underground gypsum deposits mean random sinkholes appear throughout the district, creating havoc for home owners and businesses alike.

Their main hope would appear to be in plans for the redevelopment of the former Claro Barracks, Deverell Barracks and Laver Banks area of the city. The developers' proposal includes the usual housing, retail centre, employment area and a primary school but, crucially, also lists community facilities and sports facilities. Whether that would include a possible site for the football club remains to be seen.

"We know what we want to do but when that could happen we don't know" said Camplejohn.

Should Ripon ever manage to make their dream come true, there is no guarantee they would get their preferred elevation to the NCE. Although they play in the West Yorkshire League, Northallerton Town, 17 miles to the north, are in the Northern League and ambitious North Riding Leaguers Richmond Town, 24 miles up the A1 have stated their aim is the same competition. However, slightly to the south, Knaresborough Town are in the NCE, along with Harrogate Railway Athletic.

"Yes, there's lots of teams in and around Teesside in the Northern League that would be easy for us to get to, but there's also a lot a long way away in Sunderland and up into Northumberland," said Camplejohn. "We'd much rather to stay in an area we already know."

The pleasant, tree-lined Mallorie Park ground has only a post and rail pitch surround, with no hard-standing and limited car parking. A small stand on the halfway line consist of five rows of benches with the club name emblazoned across the front. Two breeze block dug-outs complete the playing facilities, but only one was half in use for today's game with the home substitutes electing to take cover from the bright sunshine in the stand, while the visitors set up camp on the opposite touchline. The club also boasts a smart changing room block and clubhouse, complete with outdoor benches and seats. Ripon Rugby Union Club's ground is behind the stand, with a cricket ground, which has hosted Yorkshire Second XI games, further along. More sporting facilities include tennis courts at Spa Park, a short walk back towards the city centre.

Ripon City were established in 1898 and played at the cricket club before moving to Mallorie Park about the time the First World War ended, when they merged with city rivals Ripon United. That club was probably the more senior, having won the Harrogate FA Whitworth Cup in 1914 and also appeared in the FA Amateur Cup in the opening seasons of the 20th Century. They beat Rowntrees of York in their first tie in 1903 but crashed out 9-1 in a replay at York City St Clements. The following season they won 2-1 against neighbours Knaresborough but then were soundly thrashed 12-0 at South Bank.

"We've got a 1920s map of the area that shows a stand where the present one is," said Camplejohn. "We don't know if it's the same one, but if it is, it's probably like Trigger's broom in Only Fools and Horses (he famously boasted it was years old, with just a few new handles and heads along the way!)."

Since then the club has moved about local leagues in Allertonshire, York and Harrogate before merging with another local side, Yorkshire Magnets, in 1992 and progressing to the West Yorkshire League, where they have reached the heights of the Premier Division.

"We took over the club five or six years ago when it was struggling with just one men's team," said Camplejohn, who runs things alongside chairman Peter Freeman and secretary Dan Metcalfe. We had gone from the Premier Division into Division One and then Division Two in quick time. There wasn't much loyalty from the players and we decided to rebuild from the bottom. Our facilities were in a poor state; leaks in the roof and showers not working. We've all put in lots of hard work since then and our finances are in a much better state. We got a mixture of grants and funds from the Boroughbridge Landfill Tax and we're more savvy with our expenditure.

"With more teams, it means more players and more use of the clubhouse to boost funds. We've also got 28 sponsors and have had great support from local businesses helping to push us on. We want to make football as affordable for everyone as we can. All the players are local lads and have come up through the junior ranks."

City run seven teams, six of them calling Mallorie Park home. As well as the first team in the West Yorkshire League, the reserves are in the Premier Division of the Harrogate League and the development, third XI, in Division One of the same competition. There is also a Sunday side, u18s and a successful ladies team who are hopeful of promotion from the West Riding Women's League to FA Women's National League.

"Our u23s are in the West Yorkshire Floodlit League," said Camplejohn. "Their games are played at central locations on 3G pitches at Ilkley, Castleford and Bradford, among others."

The club does not have a junior section of its own but works closely with Ripon Panthers and the u18s have been set up to help bridge the gap from the u16s to adult football.

While Ripon City have hopes to move back up the league, opponents Brighouse Sports knew a win today would clinch the Division Two title – or Chairman's Summer Cup, depending on how you view the end-of-season change to fixtures after a Covid-hit campaign. The reduced 12-team competition saw each side play 11 games and Brighouse quickly showed why they were top after winning eight of their 10 games so far.

They hit the bar in the first five minutes and played some lovely passing football to pile the pressure on the home side, in front of a crowd of about 70 people. However, they could not carve out any clear opportunities and it was Ripon's Brandon Clarke who came closest to scoring after 15 minutes when his shot bounced out of goalkeeper Tom Taylor's hands before he grabbed it at the second attempt.

It looked as if the teams would turn round scoreless but seven minutes before the interval Sports took the lead with a goal out of nothing from Saxon Hargreaves, shooting from the edge of the penalty area. Liam Chippendale set up Ethan Radcliffe straight from the restart for the second half but his shot crashed against the bar from inside the six-yard box. That was only a temporary let-off for Ripon though as, within a minute, David Woffenden found the net.

It was 3-0 just after the hour mark when Luke Cranswick shot from 20 yards and the ball bounced just in front of Louis Sutcliffe to sneak underneath his dive. Kyle Fox headed against the bar at the other end after 76 minutes but this time Joel Francis was on hand to head in the rebound to pull a goal back.

Ripon pushed hard to close the gap further but could not find a way past a solid Sports defence, with the visitors coming closest to adding to the goal tally in the first minute of stoppage time. Radcliffe broke from a Ripon corner and outpaced the chasing defenders but when he pulled the ball back for an easy tap-in, he discovered he had left his teammates lagging far behind in the race upfield and the ball went harmlessly across the face of goal.

A minute later referee Martin Ohr signalled the end of the game to spark wild celebrations from the Brighouse players, which I'm sure continued on their 50-plus-mile return home on their coach.

And that was my season over. Hopes of attending the inaugural game at York City's new stadium for the York & District League Finals day were dashed at the 11th hour by car problems – another ground to add to the list for my next book, although I doubt the ticket I had already bought will still be valid…

Above - Parking the bus: Goalmouth action at Ripon.
Below - Towering tale: Ripon Cathedral peeps out from behind the clubhouse.

Champagne moment: Brighouse Sports go to town with their celebrations.

CLUB INDEX

INDEX OF CHAPTERS WITH PROFESSIONAL CLUBS MENTIONED

———————————————

Family friendly: Getting close to the action at Mexborough.

STATISTICS

Total matches seen: 31

(Four at neutral venues)

Home wins: 14

Away wins: 11

Draws: 2

Total goals scored: 136

Average: 4.39 per game

Biggest win: 6-1

Biggest aggregate:

9 – 5-4: Richmond Town v Horden CW

Goalless draws: None!

Frequency of results:

1-0	3
1-1	1
2-1	7
3-0	2
3-1	1
3-2	2
3-3	1
4-0	3
4-1	2
4-2	2
5-1	3
5-4	1
6-1	1
6-2	2

BIBLIOGRAPHY

Books

A Noble Winter's Game (Rob Grillo)

Anoraknophobia (Rob Grillo)

Denied FC (Dave Twydell)

FA Cup Complete Results (Tony Brown)

Historical Look At The Midland Counties League (David Webster)

Keighley's Soccer History (Rob Grillo)

Soap Stars & Burst Bubbles (Steven Penny)

The Best of Bradford Amateur Football (Ronnie Wharton)

The Forgotten Heroes – the story of Rawmarsh Welfare (Gary Cooper)

The Wessie: A History of the West Riding Senior FA Cup (Martin Jarred)

Tyke Travels (Steven Penny)

Newspapers/magazines

FourFourTwo

Huddersfield Examiner

Rotherham Advertiser

Sheffield Star

Wakefield Express

Yorkshire Post

Websites

Montagu Cup – www.montagucup.com

Non League Yorkshire – www.nonleagueyorkshire.com

The Busby Babe blog – www.thebusbybabe.sbnation.com

UndrTheCosh podcast – Twitter @UndrTheCosh

We Are Barnsley – www.wearebarnsley.com

plus various club and league websites

THE AUTHOR

Steven Penny is a freelance journalist, currently working as sports editor of three local newspapers – the weekly Your Local Paper in King's Lynn and monthly publications the Bridlington Echo and Thorne Times in Yorkshire. He is also a sub-editor for international travel magazine Football Weekends and The Connexion newspaper in France.

Penny has worked in journalism for more than 30 years, employed by publications including the Yorkshire Post, Hull Daily Mail, Selby Times, Bridlington Free Press and the Press Association, as well as the Eastern Daily Press, Norwich Evening News, Lynn News and Diss Express in Norfolk. He also produced his own monthly newspaper in Suffolk.

Penny published six editions of Tyke Travels – a guidebook to football in Yorkshire – plus Soap Stars and Burst Bubbles, a narrative of the 2002/03 football season.

He lives with his wife Jan, two dogs and a cat (as well as a variety of squirrels, hedgehogs and peacocks) in the West Riding of his home county, handily placed for access to all parts of the Broad Acres.

ALSO BY THIS AUTHOR

Soap Stars & Burst Bubbles
A season of Yorkshire football

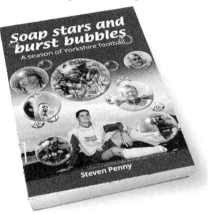

Football writer Steven Penny takes you on a journey across the football fields of Yorkshire during the 2002/03 season.

From the multi-national squad of Premiership club Middlesbrough to the six-year-old boys of Wheldrake Junior FC playing their first game.

The book concentrates on the non-League clubs of the county, from Barnoldswick – playing in Lancashire competitions – to Easington – tucked away on Spurn Point. And from Northern League sides Marske United and Northallerton Town to the world's oldest club, Sheffield FC, now based in Derbyshire.

Penny reports on more than 40 matches, including Harrogate Railway's remarkable FA Cup run and Doncaster Rovers' return to the Football League.

As well as reports and match details from every game, included are club histories, interviews with fans and club officials as well as stories from Penny's trips around the county and his long non-League football pedigree.

Got a book in you?

PUBLISHING
victorpublishing.co.uk

Printed in Great Britain
by Amazon